Cecil Torr

Memphis and Mycenae

An examination of Egyptian chronology and its application to the early

history of Greece

Cecil Torr

Memphis and Mycenae
An examination of Egyptian chronology and its application to the early history of Greece

ISBN/EAN: 9783337236588

Printed in Europe, USA, Canada, Australia, Japan

Cover: Foto ©ninafisch / pixelio.de

More available books at **www.hansebooks.com**

MEMPHIS AND MYCENÆ

AN EXAMINATION OF

EGYPTIAN CHRONOLOGY

AND ITS APPLICATION TO THE

EARLY HISTORY OF GREECE

By CECIL TORR, M.A.

Damnabitque oculos.—OVID.

CAMBRIDGE
UNIVERSITY PRESS
1896

𝕮𝖆𝖒𝖇𝖗𝖎𝖉𝖌𝖊:
PRINTED BY J. AND C. F. CLAY,
AT THE UNIVERSITY PRESS.

PREFACE.

A STATEMENT is current that the Mycenæan age in Greece can definitely be fixed at 1500 B.C., or there-abouts, on the strength of evidence from Egyptian sources. This statement is put in various forms; but that is always the substance of it. On pressure, however, it splits in two, and becomes a pair of propositions; one being that the Mycenæan age in Greece was contemporary with the reigns of certain kings of Dynasty 18 in Egypt, the other being that these kings were reigning there at some such date as 1500 B.C.

The first of these propositions is discussed here in Chapter 5. I have stated the evidence on which it rests, and pointed out the weakness of such evidence. But obviously the Mycenæan age should not be dated on the strength of evidence from Egyptian sources only. There is also a quantity of evidence from Greek sources; and that all seems to point another way. But this is not a matter that falls within the province of this book.

The second proposition is discussed in Chapters 1 to 4. I have pointed out in Chapter 4 that dates cannot be fixed by arguments about the orientation of the temples, the structure of the calendar, or the periodic rising of the dog-star that marked a Sothic cycle and the advent of a phœnix. And in Chapters 1 to 3 I have endeavoured to fix the dates in the only way in which they can be fixed with certainty: namely, by determining the true succession of the kings and the lengths of all their reigns.

T.   *b*

In such an enquiry as this the evidence is necessarily of
many different qualities. For example, an inscription on a
tomb enumerates the dignities that were conferred on the
deceased's maternal grandfather by king Se-hetep-ab-Ra
Amen-em-ha and afterwards by king Cheper-ka-Ra Usertesen, on the deceased himself by king Nub-kau-Ra Amen-
em-ha, and on his eldest son by king Cha-cheper-Ra Usertesen[a]. That gives the order in which these monarchs reigned,
but falls short of showing that they followed one another in
direct succcession. Obviously, several monarchs might have
reigned between the Cheper-ka-Ra who honoured the deceased's maternal grandfather and the Nub-kau-Ra who
honoured the deceased himself. On another tomb the inscription states that the deceased served under king Neb-
pehtet-Ra Ahmes, then under king Ser-ka-Ra Amen-hetep,
then under king Aa-cheper-ka-Ra Thothmes, then under
king Aa-cheper-en-Ra Thothmes, and then under king Men-
cheper-Ra Thothmes[b]. Here the evidence is more complete,
showing that these five monarchs followed one another in
direct succession; but it does not give the length of any of
the reigns. On another tomb, however, the inscription states
that the deceased served under king Men-cheper-Ra Thothmes
and then under king Aa-cheperu-Ra Amen-hetep; and in-
cidentally remarks that Men-cheper-Ra died on day 30 of
month 7 in year 54 of his reign, and was succeeded by
Aa-cheperu-Ra the next day[c]. There the evidence is perfect,
fixing the succession and the length of reign as well.

Sometimes the length of reign is fixed, though the succession is uncertain. In an inscription on a temple king
Heq-mat-Ra Rameses implores the gods to grant him such a
reign of 67 years as they had granted to king User-mat-Ra
Rameses[d]. That shows how long the great king reigned, but
fails to show who followed him upon the throne. Or again

[a] Tomb of Chnum-hetep at Beni Hassan. Lepsius, *Denkmaeler aus Aegypten*, part 2, plates 124, 125.

[b] Tomb of Ahmes Pen-Necheb at El-Kab. Lepsius, *ibid.*, part 3, plate 43.

[c] Tomb of Amen-em-heb at Abd el-Qurnah. *Zeitschrift fuer Aegyptische Sprache und Alterthumskunde* for 1873, page 7.

[d] Temple of Osiris at Abydos. Mariette, *Abydos*, vol. 2, plates 34, 35.

two monarchs may be placed a certain interval apart, without fixing the length of reign or the succession either. An inscription that records the death of a bull Apis in year 2 of king User-mat-Ra Pamaa, states that the beast was born in year 28 of king User-mat-Ra Sheshenk, and had attained the age of 26 years [a]. This shows that User-mat-Ra Pamaa came to the throne about 52 years after User-mat-Ra Sheshenk; but it fails to show how many years king Sheshenk may have reigned beyond the twenty-eight, or what monarchs may have reigned between him and king Pamaa.

In most cases the length of reign is only indicated roughly by a date in some inscription. Thus, for example, an inscription being dated in year 15 of king Nefer-ka-Ra Shabaka [b], the inference is that his reign extended into fifteen years at least. But such an inference may sometimes be misleading. A couple of inscriptions, when they are read together, produce a date in year 23 of king User-mat-Ra Takelot [c]; the inference being that his reign extended into three-and-twenty years at least. Yet these are the only records of him that remain; and no king of Egypt would have reigned for all those years without making himself conspicuous upon the monuments. And thus the truth may be that Takelot reigned only for a month or two, but claimed that he had lawfully been king for three-and-twenty years before, while another prince had occupied the throne.

In fact, the evidence is imperfect in so many places that no definite results can be obtained. But among the inscriptions that are discovered or deciphered every year, there usually are half-a-dozen that complete our information here and there. And no doubt the whole succession of the kings will some day be determined, together with the lengths of all their reigns, so that every event on record will be assignable to a certain date B.C.

[a] In the Serapeum Collection at the Louvre. Mariette, *Sérapéum de Memphis*, part 3, plate 26.

[b] In the British Museum. No. 24,429. Unpublished.

[c] In the Museums at Gizeh and Florence. *Recueil de travaux relatifs à la philologie et à l'archéologie Égyptiennes et Assyriennes* for 1893, pages 172—175.

Meanwhile, in spite of all its defects, this mode of fixing dates is certainly the safest mode of all; and I have therefore used it here. Possibly, I may have missed a few inscriptions that I should have quoted; and I may have quoted others incorrectly, for I have not looked at many of them myself. As a rule, I have assumed that, wherever an inscription has been published, the publication is correct; though the result of some enquiries has made me doubt the wisdom of taking all this on trust .

In default of information in inscriptions or other contemporary sources, there is Manetho's history, or what is known as such. But this is really of very little value as it

---

* For example, in the Museum at Gizeh there is a slab of stone, no. 292, with a Greek inscription on one side, and some cartouches on the other. Prof. Curtius published the Greek inscription in the *Philologische und historische Abhandlungen der k. Akademie der Wissenschaften zu Berlin* for 1854, p. 287; and he described the cartouches as " Koenigsschilder der 24sten Dynastie." Seeing that Bocchoris was the only king of the 24th Dynasty, this seems to be a scholarly way of saying that the cartouches are those of Bocchoris. Subsequently, Prof. Wachsmuth published the Greek inscription in the *Rheinisches Museum*, Neue Folge, xxviii (1873), p. 581, not knowing that it had been published before—see his note, xxx (1875), p. 640—and he said that the cartouches were those of Apries. As a matter of fact, there are two sets of cartouches placed alternately; and Prof. Curtius seems to have read the cartouches in one set as Ba-ka-Ra, and made them refer to Bocchoris, while Prof. Wachsmuth read the cartouches in the other set as Uah-ab-Ra, and made them refer to Apries. But Uah-ab-Ra is the *prænomen* of Psammitichos as well as the *nomen* of Apries, while Ba-ka-Ra is the *prænomen* of Nut-Amen. And Dr Wiedemann in his *Aegyptische Geschichte*, p. 597, has treated the cartouches as those of Psammitichos and Nut-Amen, without even mentioning any other view as possible. Yet in M. de Morgan's Gizeh Catalogue (1892, page 94) and previously in M. Maspero's Bulaq Catalogue (1883, page 381) and Mariette's Bulaq Catalogue (1876, page 91, and 1869, page 62) the cartouches are treated as those of Psammitichos and Sabakon ; so that Ba-ka-Ra must be replaced by Nefer-ka-Ra, the *prænomen* of Sabakon. In reply to an enquiry about the reading, M. Maspero very kindly sent me a note to say that Mariette and he both recognized Sabakon's name *sous les martelages*. The hieroglyphics being defaced, this reading may be questioned : but it certainly is not without a parallel, for the Berlin Museum possesses a handle of a sistrum, no. 8182, with cartouches which the catalogue describes as those of Psammitichos and Sabakon. Prof. Erman has been so good as to send me a copy; and this gives Uah-ab-Ra and Nefer-ka-Ra quite plainly. Dr Budge, however, when he was last in Egypt, did me the favour of examing the stone at Gizeh in company with Brugsch Bey ; and he tells me that they both of them read the cartouches there as Uah-ab-Ra and Haa-ab-Ra, the *nomen* and *prænomen* of Apries.

stands. The original is lost; and all the extant versions are at variance, as may be gathered from the table in this book[a]. Indeed one cannot even tell what Manetho meant by a Dynasty: and yet the division of the kings of Egypt into thirty Dynasties was the essence of his work. In any case, however, his statements would have to be received with caution; seeing that he lived in the time of the Ptolemies, when genuine materials for the early history were probably as scanty as they are to-day.

Naturally, there are some scraps of evidence from other sources; but they do not require a notice here.

Working with these materials, my conclusions are that Dynasty 18 must have begun in 1271 B.C. at latest[b], Dynasty 20 having begun in about 1000 B.C. at latest[c]; and that Dynasty 12 began in about 1500 B.C. at latest[d]. Of course, these dates are very different from those that usually are quoted; Champollion-Figeac putting the beginning of Dynasty 20 in 1279 B.C., the beginning of Dynasty 18 in 1822 B.C., and the beginning of Dynasty 12 in 3703 B.C.; Mariette putting these events in 1288 and 1703 and 3064 respectively; Brugsch putting them in 1200 and 1700 and 2466; and Lepsius in 1269 and 1591 and 2380. But in putting the beginnings of these Dynasties in 1000 and 1271 and 1500 at latest, I am not denying that earlier dates are possible. If anyone likes to put the beginning of Dynasty 18 a century before 1271 B.C., I cannot prove that he is wrong, although he cannot prove that he is right.

There being some uncertainty about these dates, there would be a difficulty in fixing the Mycenæan age in Greece by reference to Dynasty 18 in Egypt, even if the two were clearly shown to be contemporary. But after going through the evidence that is supposed to mark them as contemporary, my conclusion is simply that the Mycenæans used to trade with various tribes around Phœnicia, who had traded with the Egyptians in the time of Dynasty 18. I believe that, in

[a] At the beginning.   [b] See page 45.
[c] See page 37.   [d] See page 51.

discussing the connexion of Egypt with Greece, I have included everything that can be taken seriously; only ignoring such things as an assertion that the Greek exclamation ὦ πόποι is manifestly an invocation of the Egyptian king Pepi of Dynasty 6, and thus a proof that the Greeks knew Egypt from the earliest times[a].

In citing the inscriptions I have made the references as brief as possible; only stating where the text is published, and where the original may probably be found. And as the dates are generally B.C., I have left those letters out, unless some date A.D. is mentioned in the context. In some places I have abbreviated king User-mat-Ra Setep-en-Ra Amen-meri Rameses into king User-mat-Ra Rameses. And in transliterating all the proper names I have proceeded in a rough and ready way; my object being merely to identify the owners of the names, and not to give the force of every hieroglyph.

By permission of the Editor of the *Academy* I have re-printed here as an Appendix a note that I contributed to that journal on 27 August 1892 in connexion with a controversy that was then proceeding there. The same subject—M. Fouqué's notions as to Santorin—has since been discussed by Mr Henry S. Washington in the *American Journal of Archaeology* for 1894, vol. 9, no. 4, pp. 504–520. He had overlooked my note; but he arrived at practically the same results by somewhat different reasoning.

[a] Lauth, *Homer und Aegypten*, p. 43, *Aegyptische Chronologie*, p. 32.

C. T.

TABLE OF CONTENTS.

THE OLD CHRONICLE.

THE BOOK OF THE SOTHIS.

I.

EGYPTIAN CHRONOLOGY: DYNASTIES XXVI TO XXII.

HERODOTOS asserts that the history of Egypt was known
. accurately[a] from the time of Psammitichos onward, and he
gives the reigns as follows :—Psammitichos reigned for 54
years; then Nekos, son of Psammitichos, for 16 years; then
Psammis, son of Nekos, for 6 years; then Apries, son of
Psammis, for 25 years; then Amasis, an usurper, for 44
years; then Psammenitos, son of Amasis, for 6 months; and
then Egypt was conquered by Kambyses, king of Persia[b].
Assuming that the conquest is fixed to the year 525[c], the
dates of accession would thus be 526 for Psammenitos, 570
for Amasis, 595 for Apries, 601 for Psammis, 617 for Nekos,
and 671 for Psammitichos.

These dates are more or less confirmed by certain tombstones. The bull Apis, born on day 19 of month 6 in year
53 of king Psemtek (Psammitichos), died on day 6 of month
2 in year 16 of king Nekau (Nekos), aged 16 years 7 months
17 days[d]. Thus, year 16 of Nekos would have been year 70
of Psammitichos; so Psammitichos reigned 54 years. The
bull Apis, born on day 7 of month 2 in year 16 of king
Nekau (Nekos), died on day 12 of month 8 in year 12 of

[a] Herodotos, ii. 154. 4, ἐπιστάμεθα ἀτρεκέως.
[b] Herodotos, ii. 157, 158. 1, 159. 2, 161. 1, 169. 2, iii. 10. 1, 14. 1.
[c] Cf. Diodoros, i. 68. 6, κατὰ τὸ τρίτον ἔτος τῆς ἑξηκοστῆς καὶ τρίτης Ὀλυμπιάδος.
[d] Louvre. Catalogue de sculpture Égyptienne, no. 463.

MANETHO as quoted by EUSEBIOS.

Dyn. 11, at Thebes.
16 kings in 43 years.

Ammenemes	16

Dyn. 12, at Thebes.

Sesonchosis	46
Ammanemes	38
Sesostris	48
Lamaris	8
others	42

7 kings in 245 years.

Dyn. 13, at Thebes.
60 kings in 453 years.

Dyn. 14, at Xois.
76 kings in 184 or 484 years.

Dyn. 15, at Thebes.
? kings in 250 years.

Dyn. 16, at Thebes.
5 kings in 190 years.

Dyn. 17, of Shepherds

Saites	19
Bnon	40
Aphophis	14
Archles	30

4 kings in 103 years.

Dyn. 18, at Thebes.

Amos	?
Chebros	13
Amenophthis	21
Amensis	22
Misaphris	13
Misphragmuthosis	26
Tuthmosis	9
Amenophis	31
Oros	37
Acherres	32
Rathos	6
Chebres	12
Acherres	12
Armesses	5
Ramesses	1
Amenophath	19

16 kings in 263 years.

Dyn. 19, at Thebes.

Sethos	51
Rapsakes	61
Ammenephthes	20
Ramesses	60
Ammenemnes	5
Thuoris	7

7 kings in 209 years.

Dyn. 20, at Thebes.
12 kings in 135 years.

Dyn. 21, at Tanis.

Smendes	26
Psusennes	46
Nephelcheres	4
Amenophthis	9
Osochor	6
Psinaches	9
Psusennes	14

7 kings in 130 years.

Dyn. 18, at Thebes.

Amosis	25
Chebron	13
Amenophis	21
Miphres	12
Misphragmuthosis	26
Tuthmosis	9
Amenophis	31
Oros	36
Achencherses	16
Athoris	39
Chencheres	16
Acherres	8
Cherres	15
Armais	5
Ramesses	68
Ammenophis	40

14 kings in 348 years.

Dyn. 19, at Thebes.

Sethos	55
Rampses	66
Ammenephthes	40
Ammenemes	26
Thuoris	7

5 kings in 194 years.

Dyn. 20, at Thebes.
12 kings in 178 years.

Dyn. 21, at Tanis.

Smendis	26
Psusennes	41
Nephercheres	4
Amenophthis	9
Osochor	6
Psinaches	9
Psusennes	35

7 kings in 130 years.

I.

EGYPTIAN CHRONOLOGY: DYNASTIES XXVI TO XXII.

HERODOTOS asserts that the history of Egypt was known accurately[a] from the time of Psammitichos onward, and he gives the reigns as follows :—Psammitichos reigned for 54 years; then Nekos, son of Psammitichos, for 16 years; then Psammis, son of Nekos, for 6 years; then Apries, son of Psammis, for 25 years; then Amasis, an usurper, for 44 years; then Psammenitos, son of Amasis, for 6 months; and then Egypt was conquered by Kambyses, king of Persia[b]. Assuming that the conquest is fixed to the year 525[c], the dates of accession would thus be 526 for Psammenitos, 570 for Amasis, 595 for Apries, 601 for Psammis, 617 for Nekos, and 671 for Psammitichos.

These dates are more or less confirmed by certain tombstones. The bull Apis, born on day 19 of month 6 in year 53 of king Psemtek (Psammitichos), died on day 6 of month 2 in year 16 of king Nekau (Nekos), aged 16 years 7 months 17 days[d]. Thus, year 16 of Nekos would have been year 70 of Psammitichos; so Psammitichos reigned 54 years. The bull Apis, born on day 7 of month 2 in year 16 of king Nekau (Nekos), died on day 12 of month 8 in year 12 of

---

[a] Herodotos, ii. 154. 4, ἐπιστάμεθα ἀτρεκέως.
[b] Herodotos, ii. 157, 158. 1, 159. 2, 161. 1, 169. 2, iii. 10. 1, 14. 1.
[c] Cf. Diodoros, i. 68. 6, κατὰ τὸ τρίτον ἔτος τῆς ἑξηκοστῆς καὶ τρίτης Ὀλυμπιάδος.
[d] Louvre. Catalogue de sculpture Égyptienne, no. 463.

king Uah-ab-Ra (Apries), aged 17 years 6 months 5 days[a]. Thus, year 12 of Apries would have been year 33 of Nekos ; so Nekos and Psammis together reigned 21 years, not 22. A man, born on day 2 of month 10 in year 3 of king Nekau (Nekos), died on day 6 of month 2 in year 35 of king Ahmes (Amasis), aged 71 years 4 months 6 days[b] ; and a man, born on day 1 of month 11 in year 1 of Nekos, died on day 28 of month 8 in year 27 of Amasis, aged 65 years 10 months 2 days[c]. Thus, years 27 and 35 of Amasis would respectively have been years 67 and 75 of Nekos ; so Nekos and Psammis and Apries together reigned 40 years, not 47. Consequently, the accession of Psammitichos must be brought down from 671 to 664.

Herodotos does not vouch for Egyptian history before the accession of Psammitichos, but he gives the following account for what it may be worth :—The first king of Egypt was Men ; then, after many others, came Sesostris ; then Pheros, son of Sesostris ; then Proteus ; then Rhampsinitos ; then Cheops ; then Chephren, brother of Cheops ; then Mykerinos, son of Cheops ; then Asychis ; then Anysis ; then Sethon ; then twelve kings ruling at the same time in different parts of the country ; and then Psammitichos[d].

It is a fact that immediately before the accession of Psammitichos there were a number of kings ruling at the same time in different parts of the country ; for twenty such kings and their districts are named in the inscriptions of king Assurbanipal of Assyria[e]. And this fact is of importance in dealing with the evidence of Manetho. That author divides the kings of Egypt into thirty Dynasties, and gives each Dynasty some town or territory. So the question arises

[a] Louvre. Catalogue de sculpture Égyptienne, no. 478. Mariette, Choix de monuments du Sérapéum, plate 7.

[b] Florence Museum. Rosellini, Monumenti dell' Egitto, vol. 1, monumenti storici, plate 152.

[c] Leyden Museum. Leemans, Lettre à Salvolini, plate 25.

[d] Herodotos, ii. 99. 2, 100. 1, 102. 1, 111. 1, 112. 1, 121. 1, 124. 1, 127. 1, 129. 1, 136. 1, 137. 1, 2, 140. 1, 141. 1, 147. 2, 151, 153.

[e] British Museum. Rawlinson, Cuneiform Inscriptions, vol. 3, plate 17, lines 92-111.

whether each Dynasty ended when the next began, or whether they sometimes overlapped.

That question is settled by a tombstone. The bull Apis that died on day 21 of month 12 in year 20 of king Psemtek (Psammitichos) at the age of 21 years, was born in year 26 of king Taharqa (Tarakos)[a]. Thus, if there was any interval at all between the reigns of Psammitichos and Tarakos, the interval was less than a year. But, by Manetho's reckoning, Tarakos was the last king of Dyn. 25, and Psammitichos was the fourth or fifth king of Dyn. 26 ; Africanus making him the fourth and allowing his predecessors 21 years, while Eusebios makes him the fifth and allows them 33 years. So the earlier part of Dyn. 26 must have been concurrent with Dyn. 25.

This instance establishes the principle that Manetho's Dynasties may overlap ; and consequently upsets all those systems of chronology which are based on the assumption that each Dynasty must have ended when the next began.

Assuming that Psammitichos came to the throne in 664, Tarakos must have come to the throne in 690, as his reign lasted 26 years. Now, Assurbanipal's inscriptions say that Tarquu (Tarakos) fought against Assurbanipal himself and against Esarhaddon also[b]; and Isaiah says that Tirhakah (Tarakos) fought against Sennacherib[c]. That is all in accordance with the dates above. Sennacherib was succeeded by Esarhaddon, and Esarhaddon by Assurbanipal; and Esarhaddon seems to have reigned from 680 to 667, as stated by Ptolemy[d].

Manetho makes Tarakos the third king of Dyn. 25, making Sabakon the first and Sebichos the second ; and he makes Bocchoris the only king of Dyn. 24. Thus far the two main versions are in harmony: but Africanus allows

---

[a] Louvre. Mariette, Sérapéum de Memphis, part 3, plate 36.

[b] British Museum. Rawlinson, Cuneiform Inscriptions, vol. 3, plate 17, line 51—plate 18, line 60.

[c] Isaiah, 37. 9; cf. Kings, ii. 19. 9.

[d] Ptolemy, Canon Regnorum, 'Ασαριδίνου, ιγ', π'. Thus he reigned for 13 years ending with year 80 of the Era of Nabonassar.

40 years for Dyn. 25 and 6 years for Dyn. 24, whereas Eusebios allows 44 years for each of them. The book of the
Sothis and the Old Chronicle also give 44 years in each
case; but the Old Chronicle includes three kings in Dyn.
24 and only seven in Dyn. 26, as though two kings had
been transferred from 26 to 24. And this may indicate that
Eusebios and the Sothis have merged three reigns in one,
so that Africanus would be right in giving only 6 years to
Bocchoris.

Bocchoris reigned at least 6 years, for several inscriptions
are dated in year 6 of king Bak-en-ren-ef (Bocchoris)[a]; and
Sabakon reigned at least 15 years, for an inscription is
dated in year 15 of king Shabaka (Sabakon)[b]. Sebichos
appears to be king Shabataka; and no inscriptions are
forthcoming with dates in that king's reign. Still, if Tarakos came to the throne in 690, and Sabakon and Bocchoris
did not reign concurrently with him or with each other,
Sabakon must have come to the throne in 705 at latest
and Bocchoris in 711 at latest.

According to Manetho, Sabakon took Bocchoris prisoner
and burnt him alive[e]; but Herodotos ignores Bocchoris, and
says that Sabakon killed Nekos the father of Psammitichos[d].
This is clearly the Nechao who stands next before Psammitichos in Manetho's list of Dyn. 26, the name being Nekau in
Egyptian. His predecessors in that list are Nechepsos and
Stephinathis; and Diodoros and Plutarch make Bocchoris a
son of Tnephachthos or Technaktis, while Athenæos makes
him a son of Neochabis[e]. The names Tnephachthos, Technaktis and Stephinathis must all be variants of the Egyptian
name Tef-necht; and the names Neochabis and Nechepsos
must both be variants of some Egyptian name like Necht-abs.
Hence king Bocchoris of Dyn. 24 would seem to have been

---

[a] Louvre. Mariette, Sérapéum de Memphis, part 3, plate 34.

[b] British Museum. No. 24,429.

[e] Manetho, Fr. 65, αἰχμάλωτον Βόχχωριν ἐλὼν ἔκαυσε ζῶντα. Cf. John of
Antioch, Fr. 1. 24, οἱ δέ φασιν ὡς ἐξέδειρεν.

[d] Herodotos, ii. 152. 1.

[e] Athenæos, x. 13; Diodoros, i. 45; Plutarch, de Iside et Osiride, 8.

a son of Stephinathis or Nechepsos, the second and third kings of Dyn. 26, and either a brother of Nechao and an uncle of Psammitichos, the fourth and fifth kings of Dyn. 26, or else a brother of Nechepsos and an uncle of Nechao. And clearly there was some connexion between Dyns. 24 and 26, for Manetho assigns them both to Sais, while he assigns Dyn. 25 to Ethiopia.

Nekos or Nekau or Nechao, the fourth of the Saite kings of Dyn. 26, is obviously the Nikuu of Sais who stands at the head of the tributary kings in Assurbanipal's inscriptions[a]. He must therefore have lived on past 667; and if he was slain by Sabakon, as Herodotos asserts, Sabakon must have lived on later. And apparently Nekos and Sabakon were men of the same generation, for Nekos was the father of Psammitichos, and Psammitichos married a niece of Sabakon. The relationship is proved by three inscriptions. One shows that queen Netaqert was a daughter of king Psemtek (Psammitichos) and queen Shep-en-apet[b]. Another shows that queen Shep-en-apet was a daughter of king Pianchi and queen Amen-artas, and that queen Amen-artas was a daughter of king Kashta and queen Shep-en-apet, a daughter of king Uasarken[c]. The other shows that queen Amen-artas, the daughter of king Kashta, was the sister of king Shabaka (Sabakon)[d]. Thus, Sabakon was brother to Amen-artas, the mother of Shep-en-apet, the wife of Psammitichos.

Psammitichos was recognized at Memphis as successor to Tarakos, for the death of a bull Apis is dated in year 20 of king Psemtek (Psammitichos), while its birth is dated in year 26 of king Taharqa (Tarakos), 21 years before[e]. And similarly Sabakon must have been recognized as king before the accession of Tarakos, for the death of a bull Apis is dated in

---

[a] British Museum. Rawlinson, Cuneiform Inscriptions, vol. 3, plate 17, line 92.

[b] Assassif. Lepsius, Denkmaeler aus Aegypten, part 3, plate 270.

[c] Hermitage. Lieblein, Aegyptische Denkmaeler in St. Petersburg, pp. 6-11 and plates 1, 2.

[d] Gizeh Museum. Mariette, Karnak, plate 45. d.

[e] See above, page 3 and note a.

year 2 of king Shabaka (Sabakon)[a]. But this is not a proof that Sabakon's reign came altogether to an end when Tarakos was recognized at Memphis. In fact there is some evidence to show that his reign extended into the reign of Psammiti-chos, the cartouches of Psammitichos (Uah-ab-Ra) and Saba-kon (Nefer-ka-Ra) being carved alternately along the cornice of a shrine[b], and side by side upon the handle of a sistrum[c]. If so, the fact that Sabakon was the first king of Dyn. 25 did not prevent his reigning after Tarakos, who was the third king of Dyn. 25, and concurrently with Psammitichos, who was the fifth king of Dyn. 26.

Some cartouches with the name of king Shabaka (Sabakon) have been discovered in the ruins of Sennacherib's palace at Nineveh[d]. And curiously they are stamped upon the dark brown clay that distinguishes the archives of Assurbanipal from the archives of his predecessors. They may therefore show that Sabakon continued to be king of Egypt after Assurbanipal had become king of Assyria in 667 B.C.

In his early days Sabakon might have fought against king Sargon of Assyria. Sargon seems to have gained the throne at Babylon in 709, as stated by Ptolemy ; having gained the throne at Nineveh twelve years before, when Merodach-Bala-dan gained the throne at Babylon[e]. Now, the inscriptions in Sargon's palace say that in the second year of his reign (720) he defeated Sibi, the tartan of Egypt, and that in the seventh year of his reign (715) he imposed a tribute on Piru, the king of Egypt[f]. This Sibi is presumably the So or Seveh who

---

[a] Inscription now missing, but mentioned by Mariette, Sérapéum de Memphis, p. 184, ed. Maspero.

[b] Gizeh Museum. Catalogue, no. 292.

[c] Berlin Museum. Zeitschrift fuer Aegyptische Sprache und Alterthumskunde for 1883, p. 23.

[d] British Museum. Layard, Discoveries in the ruins of Nineveh and Babylon, p. 156.

[e] Ptolemy, Canon Regnorum, Μαρδοκεμπάδου, ιβ΄, λη΄·'Αρκεανοῦ, ε΄, μγ΄. Thus Mardokempados or Merodach-Baladan reigned at Babylon for 12 years ending with year 38 of the Era of Nabonassar, and Arkeanos or Sargon for 5 years ending with year 43.

[f] Khorsabad. Winckler, Die Keilschrifttexte Sargons. Prunkinschrift, lines 25-27. Annalen, lines 23, 27-31, 75, 97-99.

figures in the Bible as a king of Egypt[a]; for the story is that Hoshea's conspiracy with So led to the siege of Samaria by the Assyrians, and Sargon's inscriptions say that Samaria was taken in the first year of his reign[b]. But although the Bible speaks of So or Seveh as a king of Egypt, it does not call him Pharaoh; and in Sargon's inscriptions Sibi is described as tartan, or commander of the forces, while Piru (Pharaoh) is described as king. Thus, if Sibi or Seveh was Sabakon, as the likeness of the names suggests, his campaign in 720 would have preceded his accession to the throne.

Assuming that Tarakos came to the throne in 690, Sabakon must have come to the throne in 692 at latest, the death of a bull Apis being dated in the second year of his reign[c]. And strictly there is nothing to show that he came to the throne before, as the inscriptions with higher dates (such as that of year 15)[d] may all refer to his government in some outlying part of Egypt, while Tarakos was in possession of Memphis. But if he came to the throne in 692, Bocchoris must have come to the throne in 698 at latest, for the death of a bull Apis is dated in year 6 of king Bak-en-ren-ef (Bocchoris)[e].

Manetho makes Bocchoris the only king of Dyn. 24, and assigns that Dynasty to Sais, while he assigns Dyn. 23 to Tanis and makes it consist of four kings named Petubastes, Osorcho, Psammus and Zet. A king Putubisti (Petubastes) of Tanis is mentioned in Assurbanipal's list of the tributary kings[f]; but he can hardly be the Petubastes of Dyn. 23. The name Petubastes is clearly a variant of the Egyptian name Pa-ta-Bast, the masculine of Ta-ta-Bast; and a queen Ta-ta-Bast is described in an inscription as the mother of a

---

[a] Kings, ii. 17. 4. The spelling is Samech-Vau-Aleph in Hebrew, and this is represented by *Sua* in the Vulgate; but the Septuagint has Σηγώρ, with Σώας as a variant.

[b] Khorsabad. Winckler, Die Keilschrifttexte Sargons. Prunkinschrift, lines 23, 24. Annalen, lines 10–17.

[c] See above, page 6 and note a.   [d] See above, page 4 and note b.

[e] See above, page 4 and note a.

[f] British Museum. Rawlinson, Cuneiform Inscriptions, vol. 3, plate 17, line 98.

king Uasark (Osorcho)[a]. So king Petubastes of Dyn. 23
may have married his sister, as was customary; and thus
become the father of Osorcho, who succeeded him as king.
Nothing is known for certain of king Psammus or king Zet;
but the name of Psammus will perhaps supply a clue.

Names used to be repeated with little or no variation
in alternate generations of a family. And accordingly the
father and the son of Psammitichos were both called Nechao,
while his grandson was called Psammis or Psammuthis.
Hence the chances are that one of his grandfathers bore a
similar name. And if his mother was a daughter of king
Psammus of Dyn. 23, and thus transmitted the succession to
him upon the death of Zet, that would explain why he and
his successors were endowed with more authority than the
earlier kings of Dyn. 26. Moreover, Zet would then have
been contemporary with Sennacherib, as that king was
reigning till 680; and Herodotos gives Sennacherib's ant-
agonist the name of Sethon[b], which seems to be a variant
of the same Egyptian name as Zet.

Psammitichos was probably a great-grandson of Stephinathis on his father's side, as Stephinathis was the third king
before him in Dyn. 26; and if he was a grandson of
Psammus on his mother's side, he was probably a great-
grandson of Osorcho, the predecessor of Psammus in Dyn. 23.
His wife Shep-en-apet[c] was a great-granddaughter of a king
Uasarken (Osorcho) on her mother's side; and as she was a
daughter of a king Pianchi, she was possibly a great-granddaughter of another king Pianchi, the names recurring in
alternate generations. So the pedigrees suggest the notion
that Psammitichos and Shep-en-apet may both have been
descended from the king Osorcho of Dyn. 23; and that
this may be the Uasarken (Osorcho) of Bubastis who figures
with a Tef-necht (Stephinathis) of Sais in the records of
a king Pianchi, since Dyn. 23 has perhaps to be allotted to
Bubastis[d].

   [a] Louvre. Gazette Archéologique for 1880, pp. 85, 86.
   [b] Herodotos, ii. 141.
   [c] See above, page 5 and note c.   [d] See below, page 11.

Psammitichos, however, was not necessarily a great-grand-son of Stephinathis. According to Herodotos, he was a son of the elder Nekos, father of the younger Nekos, grandfather of Psammis and great-grandfather of Apries[a] : so the crown had descended from father to son for five generations, when the line was broken by the usurpation of Amasis. But there is not any proof that the elder Nekos inherited the crown as a son of Nechepsos, or Nechepsos as a son of Stephinathis. These three kings might possibly have been three brothers; and if Stephinathis had been a brother of Nekos, the father of Psammitichos, he would presumably have been contemporary with the king Pianchi who became the father-in-law of Psammitichos. But then Bocchoris seems to have been a son of Stephinathis or Nechepsos[b], and he must have come to the throne in 698 at latest[c]; so the chances are in favour of the view that Nechepsos and Stephinathis were the grandfather and great-grandfather of Psammitichos rather than his uncles.

This Stephinathis, the second of the Saite kings of Dyn. 26, is presumably the Tef-necht (Stephinathis) of Sais who headed a rebellion against a king Pianchi. In the official account of the affair[d] Pianchi is represented as the sovereign of the whole of Egypt with vassals in the various districts; and four of these vassals are described as kings, namely, Uasarken of Bubastis, Auput of Klysma, Pefaa-Bast of Heracleopolis and Nemart of Hermopolis[e]. The arch-rebel, Tef-necht of Sais, is described as great chief of the west country, prince of the cities in the Delta, royal chief of the troops, and so forth[f]; while the narrative shows that he stood nearly on a level with Pianchi himself, and made only a formal submission at the last[g]. This much being admitted in Pianchi's version of the story, one may surmise that Tef-necht was represented in his own version as sovereign of

---

[a] Herodotos, ii. 152. 1, 158. 1, 159. 2, 161. 1.

[b] See above, page 4 and note e.   [c] See above, page 7.

[d] Gizeh Museum. Mariette, Monuments divers, plates 1 to 6.

[e] Ibid., preamble and lines 1, 22, 70, 114.

[f] Ibid., lines 19, 20, 126.   [g] Ibid., lines 140–144.

the whole of Egypt with Pianchi as his vassal at Thebes, and that Manetho has acknowledged these pretensions by including him in Dyn. 26.

Pianchi cannot be identified with any of the kings in Manetho's lists; nor can any of his vassals, except Tef-necht of Sais and possibly Uasarken of Bubastis. But among these vassals there is a Sheshenk of Busiris with the title of chief of the troops, and a Pamaa of Busiris with the titles of chief of the troops and governor[a]; and they may represent the line of kings that was recognized at Memphis.

A king Aa-cheper-Ra Sheshenk was recognized at Memphis, for the death of a bull Apis is dated in year 11 of his reign[b]. He is described in the inscription as the son of king Pamaa; and a king User-mat-Ra Pamaa was recognized at Memphis, for the death of a bull Apis is dated in year 2 of his reign[c]. The death of another bull Apis is dated in year 37 of king Aa-cheper-Ra Sheshenk[d]; and the remains of this bull were discovered in the same vault with those of the bull Apis that died in year 6 of Bocchoris[e]. This indicates that these two bulls came next to one another in the divine succession, so that there could not have been any greater interval than the lifetime of a bull between year 6 of Bocchoris and year 37 of Aa-cheper-Ra Sheshenk. But the dates will also show that, as Bocchoris came to the throne in 698 at latest[f], Aa-cheper-Ra Sheshenk must have come to the throne in 735 at latest, and User-mat-Ra Pamaa in 737 at latest.

These kings Pamaa and Sheshenk would thus have been contemporaries of Pianchi, if he belonged to the third generation before Psammitichos[g]. And in that case they might reasonably be identified with his vassals at Busiris;

---

[a] Gizeh Museum. Mariette, Monuments divers, plate 2, line 18, and plate 5, line 116.

[b] Louvre. Mariette, Sérapéum de Memphis, part 3, plate 30.

[c] Louvre. Mariette, ibid., part 3, plates 26–28.

[d] Louvre. Mariette, ibid., part 3, plate 31.

[e] Mariette, ibid., pp. 175, 176, 179, 181, ed. Maspero.

[f] See above, page 7.

[g] See above, page 8.

though of course, if he was only the father-in-law of Psammitichos, the identification could not be maintained. But
whether their government was established at Busiris or
elsewhere, it seems to represent a Dynasty which Manetho
ignores. And apparently the kings of Tanis, whom Manetho
accepts for Dyns. 21 and 23, could never have been recognized at Memphis, as their names are not to be discovered
on any of the tombstones of the sacred bulls.

The two main versions of Manetho agree that Dyn. 23
belonged to Tanis and Dyn. 22 to Bubastis: but Africanus
credits Dyn. 22 with nine kings in 120 years and Dyn. 23
with four kings in 89 years, whereas Eusebios credits Dyn. 22
with only three kings and 49 years and Dyn. 23 with three
kings and 44 years. The book of the Sothis confirms the
version in Eusebios by adopting the three kings of Dyn. 22
with their 49 years, and likewise the three kings of Dyn. 23,
though it gives them 63 years in place of 44: but it puts the
kings of Dyn. 23 before the kings of Dyn. 22, and the Old
Chronicle does practically the same thing by reckoning
Dyn. 22 in place of Dyn. 23 as the Dynasty at Tanis.
These contradictions point to some confusion of Tanis with
Bubastis in the text of Manetho; and thus suggest that king
Osorcho of Dyn. 23 was actually the king Uasarken (Osorcho)
of Bubastis, who rebelled against Pianchi.

According to the Old Chronicle, there were three kings in
48 years in Dyn. 22, and two kings in 19 years in Dyn. 23;
these two Dynasties being here curtailed to 67 years in all,
whereas the book of the Sothis extends them to 112 years,
Eusebios to 93 and Africanus to 209. But then the Old
Chronicle assigns Dyn. 23 to Thebes, and ignores Bubastis
altogether; so that it may be dealing with another line of
kings, and conceivably with User-mat-Ra Pamaa and Aa-
cheper-Ra Sheshenk.

The bull Apis that died in year 2 of king User-mat-Ra
Pamaa, was born in year 28 of king User-mat-Ra Sheshenk,
and attained the age of 26 years[a]. Hence, if User-mat-Ra

---

[a] Louvre. Mariette, Sérapéum de Memphis, part 3, plate 26.

Pamaa came to the throne in 737, User-mat-Ra Sheshenk would have come to the throne in 790. An inscription is dated in year 29 of this Sheshenk[a]; so he reigned at least 29 years. But there is nothing to show that he reigned any longer; and 24 years may therefore have elapsed between his decease and the accession of Pamaa.

A certain Uasarken is mentioned in an inscription as high priest of Amen in years 22 and 26 of king User-mat-Ra Sheshenk[b]; and another inscription shows that an Uasarken, who was high priest of Amen, had a daughter named Shep-en-apet[c]. Now, the queen Shep-en-apet, who married Psammitichos, was granddaughter to a queen Shep-en-apet, who was daughter to a king Uasarken[d]. And the coincidence suggests that the high priest Uasarken may have attained the rank of king after Sheshenk's death. But as Sheshenk came to the throne in 790 at latest, Uasarken must have become high priest in 769 at latest, that is to say, more than 100 years before the accession of Psammitichos in 664. And thus Uasarken, the high priest, was possibly the grandfather of the king Uasarken whose great-granddaughter married Psammitichos.

The high priest Uasarken is described in an inscription as a son of king Hetch-cheper-Ra Takelot, and the inscription shows that he was high priest in years 11 and 15 of Takelot's reign[e]. There is not any proof that Takelot reigned for more than 15 years; and accordingly his own reign and his son's might both be placed between the reigns of User-mat-Ra Sheshenk and User-mat-Ra Pamaa, since the interval was perhaps as much as 24 years. But this could not have been the sequence, if a bull Apis died in the reign of Takelot; for a bull Apis that was born in the reign of Sheshenk, lived on

[a] Karnak. Lepsius, Denkmaeler aus Aegypten, part 3, plate 258. a.

[b] Karnak. Lepsius, ibid., part 3, plate 258. a, line 12; the pieces omitted by Lepsius being given by Maspero in the Mémoires de la Mission Archéologique Française, vol. i. pp. 741, 742.

[c] Turin Museum. Catalogue, no. 1632.

[d] See above, page 5 and note c.

[e] Karnak. Lepsius, ibid., part 3, plates 256. a, 257. a.

until the reign of Pamaa[a]. And possibly a death occurred
while Takelot was king, as a slab of stone with his cartouches
was discovered in the vaults in which the bulls were buried, and
near the slab were several tombstones bearing date in year
14 of some king's reign[b]. But this does not suffice to show
that the king was Takelot, or that the slab of stone with his
cartouches was inserted in the vaults on the occasion of a death.

In the inscription quoted above, the high priest Uasarken
is described as a son of king Takelot by his marriage with
Karamama, a daughter of the high priest Nemart, a son of
king Uasarken[c]. In another inscription, dedicated by a
certain Heru-pasen in year 37 of king Aa-cheper-Ra Sheshenk, this Heru-pasen is described as a son of Ptah-hon, a son
of Heru-pasen, a son of Ptah-hon, a son of Ptah-hetch-anch-ef,
a son of Nemart, a son of king Uasarken[d]. The same Nemart and Uasarken must be meant in both inscriptions, for
both of them call Nemart the commandant at Heracleopolis;
and it would be extraordinary if two kings of the same name
had sons of the same name holding the same appointment. So
these pedigrees will show that the younger Heru-pasen stood
three generations below Uasarken, the high priest; being in fact
his first cousin three times removed. And as this Heru-pasen
was living in year 37 of Aa-cheper-Ra Sheshenk, Uasarken
might well have become high priest by year 22 of User-mat-Ra
Sheshenk, for that was only 70 years before, if Pamaa's reign
ended in its second year. But if Takelot came before User-
mat-Ra Sheshenk instead of after him, Uasarken must have
become high priest at least 26 years earlier; and that would
make the generations of more than ordinary length.

In an inscription dedicated by a certain Pa-ta-Auset in
year 28 of king User-mat-Ra Sheshenk, this Pa-ta-Auset is
described as a son of Takelot, a son of Sheshenk, a son of
king User-mat-Ra Uasarken[e]. He was thus a second cousin

---

[a] See above, page 11 and note a.
[b] Mariette, Sérapéum de Memphis, p. 159, ed. Maspero.
[c] See above, page 12 and note e.
[d] Louvre. Mariette, ibid., part 3, plate 31.
[e] Louvre. Mariette, ibid., part 3, plate 24.

of Uasarken, the high priest, being a great-grandson of
Uasarken, the king. And as he was living in year 28 of
User-mat-Ra Sheshenk, there is no reason for supposing that
the Uasarken who was high priest in year 26 of this Sheshenk,
was a different person from the Uasarken who was high priest
in the time of Takelot and is described in Takelot's inscriptions as a great-grandson of king Uasarken. It is true that
this king Uasarken was not necessarily the User-mat-Ra
Uasarken who was great-grandfather to Pa-ta-Auset; for
neither Takelot nor Heru-pasen has given the name in full.
There may therefore have been two high priests of Amen
named Uasarken, one of whom was contemporary with a
great-grandson of king User-mat-Ra Uasarken, while the
other was himself a great-grandson of some other king
Uasarken: but that is scarcely probable.

Some inscriptions of a king Cherp-cheper-Ra Uasarken[a]
are carved upon the same gateway with the inscriptions of
kings Hetch-cheper-Ra Takelot and User-mat-Ra Sheshenk
in which an Uasarken is mentioned as high priest; and that
looks as though the high priest Uasarken may have succeeded
to the throne as Cherp-cheper-Ra. This king was presumably
of later date than Takelot and Sheshenk; the city of king
Cherp-cheper-Ra being mentioned in Pianchi's account of
the rebellion of Tef-necht[b]. But he cannot be identified with
the rebel king Uasarken of Bubastis, for the narrative shows
that his city was in another part of Egypt; nor yet with the
Osorcho of Dyn. 23, as that Osorcho was preceded by a
Petubastes. Possibly, he was the father of Pa-ta-Bast, or
Petubastes; and thus a progenitor of Shep-en-apet and
Psammitichos in the fifth generation[c].

Adjoining these inscriptions of kings Cherp-cheper-Ra
Uasarken, User-mat-Ra Sheshenk and Hetch-cheper-Ra
Takelot are those of a king Hetch-cheper-Ra Sheshenk[d];

---

[a] Karnak. Lepsius, Denkmaeler aus Aegypten, part 3, plate 257. b, c.

[b] Gizeh Museum. Mariette, Monuments divers, plate 1, line 4, and plate 4,
line 77.

[c] See above, page 8.

[d] Karnak. Lepsius, ibid., part 3, plates 253. b, c, 254. a, b, 255. a, b.

and the position of his cartouches marks him as the builder of the gateway. He must therefore have reigned before the other three : but User-mat-Ra Uasarken may have reigned before him, as that king's inscriptions are carved upon another building.

The pedigree of Heru-pasen[a] runs straight on through Nemart and his wife Tent-sepeh to king Uasarken and his wife Mut-hetch-anch-es. But then it breaks off, and names a king Takelot with his wife Kapes, a king Uasarken with his wife Ta-meh-Chensu, and a king Sheshenk with his wife Karamata. And then it breaks off again, starting afresh with Nemart and his wife Tent-sepeh, and running on through a Sheshenk and his wife Meht-en-usech and three more genera-tions of private persons to Tehen-buiuaua, the founder of the family.

This must mean that Nemart was really a son of Sheshenk, and only an adopted son of king Uasarken. And the pedi-gree does not give him the title of royal son ; but it gives his mother Meht-en-usech the title of royal mother, and it gives his son Ptah-hetch-anch-ef the title of royal son, so that his position must have been abnormal. In the first section of the pedigree he is described as a personage of the same rank, the rank being specified above in connexion with the younger Ptah-hon, who had the title of governor, commander of the south country, commander of the priests at Heracleopolis and commander of the forces ; but in the third section Nemart has the title of great chief, and his ancestors are described as personages of the same rank. These statements are con-firmed by two inscriptions of earlier date. One of these describes Nemart, the son of king Uasarken, as high priest of Amen, commander of the forces at Heracleopolis and governor[b]; and the other describes Nemart, the son of Sheshenk and Meht-en-usech, as great chief of the troops and chief among chiefs[c]. The explanation may be that Nemart inherited one set of titles from Sheshenk, and acquired the other

[a] See above, page 13 and note d.
[b] Karnak. Lepsius, Denkmaeler aus Aegypten, part 3, plate 257. a.
[c] Gizeh Museum. Mariette, Abydos, vol. 2, plate 37, line 17.

set from Uasarken on adoption; but could not use his ancestral titles as an adopted son, or the others as his father's son.

In order to maintain the notion that the pedigree runs straight on from Heru-pasen to Tchen-buiuaua in the fifteenth generation, one must suppose that there are eight mistakes in an inscription which otherwise is accurate, and that these eight mistakes are all consistent with each other. Thus, for example, the supposition is that the titles of royal son and royal mother are given by mistake to the son of Nemart in the fourth generation and to the mother of Nemart in the eleventh. If so, the scribe must have made two mistakes of exactly the same kind in relation to two men of the same name with wives of the same name ; and that does not seem likely".

If the pedigree is divided into sections, the three kings in the second section must be collateral ancestors of Heru-pasen. And as they share the title of royal son with Ptah-hetch-anch-ef, who was a son of Nemart, the presumption is that they were also sons of Nemart.

The names of these three kings, Sheshenk, Uasarken and Takelot, are clearly the equivalents of the names Sesonchis, Osorthon and Takelothis, which Manetho inserts in Dyn. 22. But here the two main versions are at variance ; for Eusebios confines the Dynasty to three kings, whereas Africanus enlarges it to nine, reckoning Sesonchis and Osorthon as the first and second and Takelothis as the sixth, but never mentioning the names of the additional kings. If king Hetch-cheper-Ra Takelot came sixth, those three kings in the pedigree might have come next after him or next before, as they probably were Nemart's sons, and he was Nemart's son-in-law. But possibly they were only vassal kings, not counted in the Dynasty ; for the pedigree reserves the title of lord of the entire country for the king Uasarken who was father to Nemart.

Africanus may perhaps have counted Cherp-cheper-Ra

* Lepsius corrected the eight alleged mistakes ; and his version of the text is often quoted as though it were the original—for instance, by Wiedemann in his Aegyptische Geschichte, vol. 2, pp. 542 ff.

Uasarken, User-mat-Ra Pamaa and Aa-cheper-Ra Sheshenk as the last three kings of Dyn. 22; and thus joined that Dynasty to 24 and 25, leaving 23 aside. This is probably the succession that was recognized at Memphis[a]: and curiously Africanus and Eusebios agree about the length of time from Takelothis to the end of 25, when 23 is skipped; Eusebios allowing 44 years apiece for Dyns. 24 and 25, while Africanus allows 40 years for Dyn. 25, 6 for 24, and 42 for these additional kings, or 88 in all. They both allow 13 years for Takelothis, and thus would make him king from 765 to 752, if Dyn. 25 came to an end in 664[b]. And the chances are that Hetch-cheper-Ra Takelot was king about that time, if he was the successor of User-mat-Ra Sheshenk; for that king came to the throne in 790 at latest, and reigned at least 29 years[c].

The death of a bull Apis is dated in year 23 of king User-mat-Ra Uasarken[d]; so that he must have come to the throne in 813 at latest, User-mat-Ra Sheshenk having come to the throne in 790 at latest. But if the death of a bull Apis was dated in year 14 of king Hetch-cheper-Ra Takelot[e], that king must have come to the throne in 804 at latest, and Uasarken in 827 at latest.

An inscription bears date in year 21 of king Hetch-cheper-Ra Sheshenk[f]: so this Sheshenk reigned at least 21 years, and he reigned before User-mat-Ra Sheshenk and Hetch-cheper-Ra Takelot[g]. He might have reigned concurrently with User-mat-Ra Uasarken: but if he reigned before, he must have come to the throne in 834 or 848 at latest, according to the place assigned to Takelot; and if he reigned after, he must have come to the throne in 811 or 825 at latest, and Uasarken in 834 or 848 at latest. To judge by the

---

[a] See above, page 10, and also pages 5 and 7.
[b] See above, page 3.　　　　　　　[c] See above, page 12.
[d] Louvre. Catalogue de la Salle Historique, no. 275. Cf. Mariette, Sérapéum de Memphis, p. 158, ed. Maspero.
[e] See above, page 13.
[f] Silseleh. Lepsius, Denkmaeler aus Aegypten, part 3, plate 254. c.
[g] See above, pp. 14, 15.

generations in the pedigrees[a], both these Sheshenks would
have reigned between Uasarken and Takelot. In that case
Uasarken would have come to the throne at least 65 years
before his great-grandson Uasarken was high priest in year
22 of king User-mat-Ra Sheshenk, and 71 years before his
great-grandson Pa-ta-Auset dedicated the inscription in year
28; and at least 135 years before his great-grandson Ptah-hon's
great-grandson Heru-pasen dedicated the inscription in year 37
of king Aa-cheper-Ra Sheshenk.

Manetho makes Osorthon the successor of Sesonchis in
Dyn. 22; but possibly the names have been transposed. And
if User-mat-Ra Uasarken (Osorthon) was the first king of
the Dynasty, while Hetch-cheper-Ra Sheshenk (Sesonchis)
was the second, and Hetch-cheper-Ra Takelot (Takelothis)
was the sixth[b], the intervening kings may have been User-
mat-Ra Sheshenk, an User-mat-Ra Auaput[c] who probably
was a son of Hetch-cheper-Ra Sheshenk[d], and an User-
mat-Ra Takelot[e] who cannot reasonably be placed elsewhere.
These three kings are omitted by Eusebios; and Africanus
allows them only 25 years altogether. But an inscription
is dated in year 29 of king User-mat-Ra Sheshenk[f], and
another seems to be dated in year 23 of king User-mat-
Ra Takelot[g]; so that the three reigns would have taken more
than 52 years, unless they overlapped. Very probably,
however, User-mat-Ra Auaput and User-mat-Ra Takelot
reigned concurrently with User-mat-Ra Sheshenk, as there is
nothing to indicate that either of them was recognized as
king at Memphis or at Thebes.

Including these three kings, Africanus allows 61 years
from the accession of Takelothis to the accession of Sesonchis
at the beginning of Dyn. 22; while Eusebios allows 36 years
for the same period, these kings being excluded. And thus,

[a] See above, pp. 12, 13.   [b] See above, pp. 16, 17.
[c] Gizeh Museum. Naville, The Mound of the Jew, plate 1.
[d] See below, page 24.
[e] Gizeh Museum. Recueil de travaux for 1893, vol. 15, pp. 172, 173.
[f] See above, page 12 and note a.
[g] Florence Museum. Recueil de travaux, ibid., p. 175.

if Takelothis came to the throne in 765, the Dynasty would either have begun in 801 or else in 826, whereas the inscriptions are in favour of the dates of 811 or 834 at latest[a].

In one of his inscriptions king Hetch-cheper-Ra Sheshenk has given a list of the cities that he captured[b]; and this includes a number of cities in Palestine and Syria. So this Sheshenk is probably the Shishak, king of Egypt, who figures in the Bible as the assailant of Jerusalem in year 5 of Rehoboam[c].

Now, the Bible says that Rehoboam reigned for 17 years, then Abijam for 3 years, then Asa for 41 years, then Jehosaphat for 25 years, then Jehoram for 8 years, then Ahaziah for 1 year, then Athaliah for 6 years, then Joash for 40 years, then Amaziah for 29 years, then Azariah for 52 years, then Jotham for 16 years, then Ahaz for 16 years, and then Hezekiah; and Samaria was taken in year 6 of Hezekiah[d]. Assuming that Samaria was taken in 721[e], the dates of accession would thus be 726 for Hezekiah, 742 for Ahaz, 758 for Jotham, 810 for Azariah, 839 for Amaziah, 879 for Joash, 885 for Athaliah, 886 for Ahaziah, 894 for Jehoram, 919 for Jehosaphat, 960 for Asa, 963 for Abijam, and 980 for Rehoboam. And thus Shishak's invasion would fall in 976.

But the Bible also says that Rehoboam and Jeroboam began their reigns together; and Jeroboam reigned for 22 years, then Nadab for 2 years, then Baasha for 24 years, then Elah for 2 years, then Zimri for a week, then Omri for 12 years, then Ahab for 22 years, then Ahaziah for 2 years, then Joram for 12 years, then Jehu for 28 years, then Jehoahaz for 17 years, then Jehoash for 16 years, then Jeroboam for 41 years, then Zachariah for six months, then Shallum for one month, then Menahem for 10 years, then Pekahiah for 2 years, then Pekah for 20 years, and then Hoshea; and Samaria was taken

---

[a] See above, page 17.
[b] Karnak. Lepsius, Denkmaeler aus Aegypten, part 3, plates 252, 253. a.
[c] Chronicles, ii. 12. 2–4; Kings, i. 14. 25.
[d] Kings, i. 14. 21, 31, 15. 2, 8, 10, 24, 22. 42, 50, ii. 8. 17, 24, 26, 11. 1–3, 21, 12. 1, 21, 14. 2, 21, 15. 2, 7, 33, 38, 16. 2, 20, 18. 10.
[e] See above, pp. 6, 7.

in year 9 of Hoshea[a]. Again assuming that Samaria was
taken in 721, the dates of accession would thus be 729 for
Hoshea, 749 for Pekah, 751 for Pekahiah, 761 for Menahem,
802 for Jeroboam, 818 for Jehoash, 835 for Jehoahaz, 863 for
Jehu, 875 for Joram, 877 for Ahaziah, 899 for Ahab, 911 for
Omri, 913 for Elah, 937 for Baasha, 939 for Nadab, and 961
for Jeroboam. And thus Shishak's invasion would fall in
957.

Both sets of figures are adopted by Josephus, except that
he places the taking of Samaria in year 7 of Hezekiah, and
gives 27 years to Jehu and 40 to the younger Jeroboam[b].
Shishak's invasion would thus fall in 977 and 955.

Unfortunately, nothing can be gained by comparing the
Bible with the Assyrian inscriptions. Menahem of Samaria
is named in Tiglath Pileser's inscriptions as a tributary in year
8, and Azariah of Judah as a rebel in year 7[c]. The lists of
Eponyms show that Tiglath Pileser came to the throne 24
years before Sargon[d]; and thus in 745, if Samaria was taken
in 721, for Sargon took the city in the first year of his reign[e].
Consequently, Menahem and Azariah must have been alive in
738 and 739, although the Bible puts their deaths in 751 and
758. Ahab of Samaria can hardly be identified with an Ahab
of Sirhala in Shalmaneser's inscriptions; or Jehu of Samaria,
who was a son of Jehosaphat, with a Jehu, son of Omri, whose
country is not named[f]. Shalmaneser mentions this Ahab in
year 6 and this Jehu in year 18, whereas the Bible requires
an interval of 14 years at least, since it makes Ahab reign

---

[a] Kings, i. 12. 1, 20, 14. 20, 15. 25, 28, 33, 16. 6, 8, 10, 15, 16, 23, 28, 29, 22.
40, 51, ii. 1. 17, 3. 1, 9. 24, 10. 35, 36, 13. 1, 9, 10, 13, 14. 23, 29, 15. 8, 10, 13,
14, 17, 22, 23, 25, 27, 30, 18. 10.

[b] Josephus, de antiquitatibus Judaicis, viii. 8. 1, 3, 10. 2, 4, 11. 3, 4, 12. 3–6,
13. 1, ix. 2. 1, 2, 3. 2, 5. 3, 6. 3, 7. 1, 2, 8. 1, 4–6, 9. 3, 10. 1, 4, 11. 1, 12. 1, 3,
14. 1.

[c] British Museum. Rawlinson, Cuneiform Inscriptions, vol. 3, plate 9, lines
2, 3, 10, 22, 23, 31, 50.

[d] British Museum. Rawlinson, ibid., vol. 3, plate 1, col. 4, line 26—col. 5,
line 5.

[e] See above, pp. 6, 7.

[f] British Museum. Rawlinson, ibid., vol. 3, plate 5, lines 64, 65, plate 8,
lines 91, 92; Layard, Inscriptions in the Cuneiform Character, plate 98, line 2.

from 899 to 877 and Jehu from 863 to 835. Moreover, the lists of Eponyms show that Shalmaneser came to the throne 115 years before Tiglath Pileser[a]; and thus in 860, if this section of the lists is trustworthy. But that seems doubtful, as these 115 years include the reigns of several kings whose existence is not attested by the monuments.

The difficulties are increased by other statements in the Bible. It says that Pekah was succeeded by Hoshea; and that Ahaz began to reign in year 17 of Pekah, and was succeeded by Hezekiah in year 3 of Hoshea[b]. Hence, if Ahaz reigned for 16 years, Pekah must have reigned for 30; or if Pekah reigned for 20, Ahaz must have reigned for 6. Again, it says that Amaziah was succeeded by Azariah; and that Jeroboam began to reign in year 15 of Amaziah, and was succeeded by Zachariah in year 38 of Azariah[c]. Hence, if Jeroboam reigned for 41 years, Amaziah must have reigned for 18; or if Amaziah reigned for 52, Jeroboam must have reigned for 75. And so forth.

Thus the numerals in the Bible appear to be corrupt. In other respects its statements may be credible: but they are hardly of a nature to outweigh the evidence from Egyptian sources about the date of Shishak, if Shishak is intended for Hetch-cheper-Ra Sheshenk. In the Septuagint, however, the invader's name is given as Susakim; and the book of the Sothis puts Susakim where Manetho puts Smendes, thus transferring the invasion from the early years of Dyn. 22 to the early years of 21.

[a] British Museum. Rawlinson, Cuneiform Inscriptions, vol. 3, plate 1, col. 2, line 6—col. 4, line 26.

[b] Kings, ii. 15. 30, 16. 1, 20, 18. 1.   [c] Kings, ii. 14. 19–21, 23, 29, 15. 8.

EGYPTIAN CHRONOLOGY: DYNASTIES XXII TO XX.

A king Sheshenk, who was also high priest of Amen, is described in an inscription as a son of king Uasarken by his marriage with Mat-ka-Ra, a daughter of king Pasebchanu[a]. There is nothing on the face of the inscription to indicate which Sheshenk is meant: but Aa-cheper-Ra Sheshenk may be dismissed, as he was a son of king Pamaa[b].

In the mummy of Nesi-Chensu the high priest Pinetchem is described as a son of king Pasebchanu, and also as a son of Men-cheper-Ra[c]; and in his own mummy he is described as a son of Men-cheper-Ra, a son of king Pinetchem[d]. In other inscriptions Pasebchanu has the royal cartouche with the title of high priest[e]; and so also has Men-cheper-Ra[f]. And as Men-cheper-Ra is one of the names that must stand first, while Pasebchanu is one of those that must stand second, the presumption is that there was a Men-cheper-Ra Pasebchanu, who was himself high priest and king, and was the father of Pinetchem the high priest, and a son of Pinetchem the king.

[a] British Museum. Lepsius, Auswahl, plate 15.

[b] See above, page 10.

[c] Gizeh Museum. Maspero, Les momies royales de Déir el-Bahari, in the Mémoires de la Mission Archéologique Française, vol. 1, p. 579.

[d] Gizeh Museum. Maspero, ibid., p. 572.

[e] Saurma Collection. Zeitschrift fuer Aegyptische Sprache und Alterthums-kunde for 1882, p. 88.

[f] Berlin Museum. Lepsius, Denkmaeler aus Aegypten, part 3, plate 251. k.

The king Pinetchem is called Pinetchem on an outer wrapping of his mummy, and Cha-cheper-Ra on the bandages inside[a]; and his name Cha-cheper-Ra Pinetchem is given in full on the boxes for his Osirian figures[b]. Two sons of this Pinetchem became high priests of Amen as well as Men-cheper-Ra Pasebchanu; for the high priest Masahart is described upon his coffin as a son of king Pinetchem[c], and on another coffin the deceased is described as a son of the high priest Tchet-Chensu-af-anch, a son of Pinetchem the high priest and king[d].

In the inscriptions on the temple of Chensu this Pinetchem appears as king and also as high priest; and here he is described as a son of the high priest Pianchi[e]. This is presumably the Pianchi who appears here as the eldest son of Her-Heru[f]: but possibly it may be that Pianchi's grandfather, the name recurring in alternate generations. As for Her-Heru, he has the royal cartouche with the title of high priest in most of these inscriptions[g]; but he also appears here simply as high priest in attendance on king Men-mat-Ra Rameses[h].

Thus the succession of high priests of Amen can be traced through several generations. Under king Men-mat-Ra Rameses the office was held by Her-Heru, who afterwards was king. From him it may have passed to his eldest son Pianchi, and then to Pianchi's son Pinetchem, who was also king. But possibly Pinetchem and Her-Heru were both the sons of a Pianchi who held the office before the time of Her-Heru. From Pinetchem it passed to three of his sons, Tchet-Chensu-af-anch, Masahart and Pasebchanu, the last of whom was also king. And from Pasebchanu it passed to

[a] Gizeh Museum. Maspero, Les momies royales de Déir el-Bahari, in the Mémoires de la Mission Archéologique Française, vol. 1, pp. 570, 788.

[b] Gizeh Museum. Maspero, ibid., pp. 590, 788.

[c] Gizeh Museum. Maspero, ibid., p. 571.

[d] Inscription now missing: see below, page 63 and note d.

[e] Karnak. Lepsius, Denkmaeler aus Aegypten, part 3, plates 248. h, 249. a, b, d, 250. a, c, 251. a, b, c.

[f] Ibid., plate 247. a, and Lepsius, Koenigsbuch, no. 533.

[g] Ibid., plates 243. a, b, 244. a, 245. b, c, 246. a, b, 248. a.

[h] Ibid., plate 238. b.

his son Pinetchem, and then (through the marriage of his daughter Mat-ka-Ra with a king Uasarken) to his grandson Sheshenk, who was also king.

Some inscriptions of king User-mat-Ra Uasarken[a] are carved upon the temple of Chensu with the inscriptions of these high priests and kings: and this suggests that he was the Uasarken who married the heiress of the family. In an inscription from another part of Egypt his queen's name is given as Karama[b]; and that is possibly a variant of Mat-ka-Ra, for the difference is only in the composition of the hieroglyphs. But several of his wives may have had the rank of queen.

In the inscriptions of king Hetch-cheper-Ra Sheshenk his son Auput or Aupuat is mentioned as high priest of Amen[c]; and if this was the Sheshenk who became high priest by virtue of his ancestry, the office would naturally have descended to his son. There is also an inscription of king User-mat-Ra Auaput[d]: and that looks as though this high priest had succeeded his father on the throne as well.

Auput is mentioned in an inscription as high priest of Amen in year 21 of king Hetch-cheper-Ra Sheshenk[e]; and in other inscriptions a certain Auapuat is entitled a royal son of Rameses[f], while the title of royal son of Rameses is given to the high priest of Amen in year 28 of some king Sheshenk[g]. This seems to show that the name Auapuat is merely a variant of the name Auput, Auaput or Aupuat; and that the high priest Auput, the son of king Hetch-cheper-Ra Sheshenk, is the personage with the title of royal son of Rameses. The same title is given to two dignitaries named Tchet-Heru-af-

---

[a] Karnak. Lepsius, Denkmaeler aus Aegypten, part 3, plate 258. c; Champollion, Monuments de l'Égypte, notices, vol. 2, pp. 240 ff., nos. 5, 8.

[b] British Museum. Naville, Bubastis, plate 42.

[c] Karnak. Lepsius, ibid., part 3, plates 253. b, c, 255. a, b.

[d] Gizeh Museum. Naville, The Mound of the Jew, plate 1.

[e] Silseleh. Lepsius, ibid., part 3, plate 254. c.

[f] Gizeh Museum. Maspero, Les momies royales de Déir el-Baharî, in the Mémoires de la Mission Archéologique Française, vol. 1, p. 719.

[g] Berlin Museum. Zeitschrift fuer Aegyptische Sprache und Alterthumskunde for 1883, p. 10.

anch,[a] and Tchet-Ptah-af-anch[b] in two inscriptions dating from the reign of Hetch-cheper-Ra Sheshenk; and in another it is given to a Nemart, whose mother is styled Panrashnes, the daughter of the great chief[c]. Thus, in two of the five cases in which the title is employed, it seems to be given to a son of Hetch-cheper-Ra Sheshenk, while in two others it certainly is given to people who were living in his time. So the probabilities are that he assumed the name of Rameses; and such an act would mean that he came close to Men-mat-Ra Rameses, or else to Cheper-mat-Ra Rameses[d], who was perhaps that king's successor.

The high priest Auput's name appears on the bandages in the mummy of Tchet-Ptah-af-anch with the date of year 10 of king Hetch-cheper-Ra Sheshenk, and perhaps of year 5 also[e]. And this mummy was found with a number of others that bear endorsements by the younger Pinetchem and his predecessors back to Her-Heru. This seems to indicate that Auput should be included in this family of priests; and that his father Hetch-cheper-Ra Sheshenk may therefore be identified with the Sheshenk whose mother was Pinetchem's sister.

This Pinetchem's name appears with the date of year 3 on a bandage in the mummy of Nesi-Chensu[f], and with the dates of years 7 and 9 and perhaps of years 1 and 3 on the bandages in his own mummy[g]; while other inscriptions show that he was buried in year 16, and Nesi-Chensu in year 5[h]. These dates appear to belong to the reign of king Amen-em-Apt; for a couple of inscriptions on the mummies mention this Pinetchem, the son of Pasebchanu, as high

[a] Posno Collection. Mariette, Monuments divers, plate 63. a.

[b] Gizeh Museum. Maspero, Les momies royales de Déir el-Bahari, in the Mémoires de la Mission Archéologique Française, vol. I, p. 573.

[c] Miramar Castle. Zeitschrift fuer Aegyptische Sprache und Alterthumskunde for 1890, pp. 36 ff.

[d] Bab el-Moluk. Lepsius, Denkmaeler aus Aegypten, part 3, plate 239. b.

[e] Gizeh Museum. Maspero, ibid., p. 573.

[f] Gizeh Museum. Maspero, ibid., p. 579.

[g] Gizeh Museum. Maspero, ibid., p. 572.

[h] Der el-Bahari. Maspero, ibid., pp. 520—523.

priest with Amen-em-Apt as king[a]. And this Amen-em-Apt is presumably the king whose name is elsewhere given in full as User-mat-Ra Amen-em-Apt[b] with the pair of epithets, Setep-en-Amen and Amen-meri, which had previously been adopted by king Cha-cheper-Ra Pinetchem[c].

But there is also an endorsement by a high priest named Pinetchem on the shroud of king User-mat-Ra Rameses, and this is dated in year 17[d]; so that, if this belongs to the Pinetchem who died in year 16 of king Amen-em-Apt, it must date from the reign of that king's predecessor. This inscription says that in year 17 the high priest Pinetchem repaired the coffin of king User-mat-Ra Rameses in the tomb of king Men-mat-Ra Seti; but an inscription on the coffin itself says that in year 16 the coffin was removed from the tomb of king Men-mat-Ra Seti to the cemetery of king Amen-hetep[e], while similar inscriptions on the coffins of king Men-mat-Ra Seti and king Men-pehtet-Ra Rameses show that the date in year 16 refers to the reign of king Se-Amen[f]. Most probably the coffins were taken over there in year 16 of king Se-Amen, and brought back again next year; for subsequent inscriptions on the coffins of kings User-mat-Ra Rameses and Men-mat-Ra Seti show that they were taken over there again in year 10[g]. This last date must refer to the reign of king Amen-em-Apt, since the removal was conducted by the treasurer Tchet-Chensu-af-anch who conducted the funerals of Nesi-Chensu and Pinetchem in years 5 and 16 of that king's reign; and with him was the priest Aunnefer who was also with him at the funeral of Pinetchem. Apparently, the previous removal occurred a very little while before, as that was conducted by the priest Anch-af-en-Amen

---

[a] Wiedemann Collection. Zeitschrift fuer Aegyptische Sprache und Alterthumskunde fur 1882, p. 86.

[b] Berlin Museum. Zeitschrift &c. for 1882, plate 1, no. 6. Gizeh Museum. Mariette, Monuments divers, plate 102. b.

[c] Gizeh Museum. Maspero, Les momies royales de Déir el-Bahari, in the Mémoires de la Mission Archéologique Française, vol. 1, pp. 590, 788.

[d] Gizeh Museum. Maspero, ibid., p. 560.   [e] Ibid., p. 558.

[f] Gizeh Museum. Maspero, ibid., pp. 551, 553, and plates 10. a, 12.

[g] Ibid., pp. 554, 559, and plate 12.

who was with Tchet-Chensu-af-anch at the funeral of Nesi-Chensu; and he was assisted by the engineer and scribe Nesi-paqashutu who assisted Tchet-Chensu-af-anch at the funerals of Nesi-Chensu and Pinetchem. And clearly the removal cannot have occurred before the time of Her-Heru, seeing that his name appears in earlier inscriptions on these coffins[a].

The high priest Her-Heru adopted the epithet Se-Amen in his cartouche as king[b]; and thus he might be credited with the dates in year 16 of king Se-Amen. But elsewhere king Se-Amen's name is given in full as Nutar-cheper-Ra Se-Amen with the epithets Setep-en-Amen and Amen-meri[c]: and that seems to distinguish him from Her-Heru.

The younger Pinetchem's father, the high priest Men-cheper-Ra, has put his name upon a bandage in the mummy of king Men-mat-Ra Seti with the date of year 6[d]; and this may refer to the reign of king Se-Amen. But another inscription shows that Men-cheper-Ra was high priest in year 25[e]; and if his son had become high priest by year 17 of king Se-Amen, that must refer to the reign of Se-Amen's predecessor. In this inscription Men-cheper-Ra is called a son of king Pinetchem; and thus the date is probably in that king's reign. Similarly, the high priest Masahart is called a son of king Pinetchem in an endorsement on the coffin of king Ser-ka-Ra Amen-hetep with the date of year 16[f]: so this may also refer to that reign. And the name of king Cha-cheper-Ra Pinetchem himself appears on a wrapping of the mummy of king Neb-pehtet-Ra Ahmes with the date of year 8[g], which is presumably of his own reign.

---

[a] Gizeh Museum. Maspero, Les momies royales de Déir el-Bahari, in the Mémoires de la Mission Archéologique Française, vol. 1, pp. 553, 557, and plates 10. b, 12.

[b] Karnak. Lepsius, Denkmaeler aus Aegypten, part 3, plates 243. a, b, 244. a, b, 245. b, c, 246. a, b, c, 248. a.

[c] Gizeh Museum. Petrie, Tanis, vol. 2, plate 8.

[d] Gizeh Museum. Maspero, ibid., p. 555.

[e] Louvre. Brugsch, Reise nach der Grossen Oase, plate 22.

[f] Gizeh Museum. Maspero, ibid., p. 536.

[g] Gizeh Museum. Maspero, ibid., p. 534.

This all seems to indicate that king Pinetchem was
officiating in year 8, while his son Masahart filled the office
of high priest in year 16, and his son Men-cheper-Ra in year
25 of this reign and year 6 of the next; and that the younger
Pinetchem, the son of Men-cheper-Ra, was high priest in year
17 of that reign, and retained the office till his death in year
16 of the reign after.   Apparently, king Pinetchem was
succeeded by kings Se-Amen and Amen-em-Apt: yet Men-
cheper-Ra became a king as Pasebchanu, and married his
daughter Mat-ka-Ra to a king Uasarken.   And accordingly
one line of succession must have run from Cha-cheper-Ra
Pinetchem through Nutar-cheper-Ra Se-Amen to User-mat-
Ra Amen-em-Apt, while another ran through Men-cheper-Ra
Pasebchanu to Mat-ka-Ra and her son Hetch-cheper-Ra
Sheshenk by her marriage with User-mat-Ra Uasarken or
some other king of that name.   And this Sheshenk seems to
have called himself a Rameses, as though he claimed the
heritage of Men-mat-Ra Rameses or Cheper-mat-Ra Rameses,
whichever of them was the last king of that family.

The two direct lines of succession may proceed from the
two queens, Mat-ka-Ra and Hent-taiu, who are represented
with king Pinetchem in the temple of Chensu[a].   These
queens are honoured with the royal cartouche in places where
their husband has nothing but the title of high priest; and
this seems to indicate that the crown was claimed through
them.   In a papyrus of her own, queen Hent-taiu is called a
daughter of queen Tent-Amen and Nebseni, a counsellor[b].
But nothing is known of queen Tent-Amen; nor is there any
record of the parents of queen Mat-ka-Ra.   Pinetchem was
himself a grandson, or possibly a brother, of the high priest
Her-Heru who certainly was king[c]: yet the superior rank of
both his wives suggests that they were members of a greater
family, and perhaps the heiresses of Rameses.

[a] Karnak.   Lepsius, Denkmaeler aus Aegypten, part 3, plate 250. a, b, c: cf.
plate 249. f.
[b] Gizeh Museum.   Mariette, Les papyrus Égyptiens du Musée de Boulaq, vol.
3, plates 16, 17.
[c] See above, page 23.

Mat-ka-Ra was probably the mother of Pinetchem's son, king Pasebchanu; for names were repeated in alternate generations, and Pasebchanu's daughter was called Mat-ka-Ra. In a decree which places the possessions of this Mat-ka-Ra under the protection of the Trinity at Thebes, they are specified as those which she brought with her when she came to the south country, and those which were presented to her there[a]. And this must mean that her father Pasebchanu was king of the north country, or Delta, while her husband Uasarken resided in the south country, or valley of the Nile. Possibly, the kings Se-Amen and Amen-em-Apt were son and grandson of Pinetchem by his marriage with Hent-taiu, and inherited the south country while Pasebchanu inherited the north.

Seeing that king Pinetchem's father was named Pianchi[b], one may surmise that some of his descendants also bore this name; and that the house of Se-Amen and Amen-em-Apt may be represented by the king Pianchi who subdued the rebellion of Tefnecht[c], and the king Pianchi who was father-in-law to Psammitichos[d]. And as the inscriptions of these later kings have mostly come from Ethiopia, this family might possibly include king Ammeris the Ethiopian, whom Eusebios places at the head of Dyn. 26; the name Ammeris being probably a variant of Amen-meri, which ranges with such names as Se-Amen and Amen-em-Apt.

According to Manetho, Dyn. 21 consisted of seven kings named Smendes, Psusennes, Nephercheres, Amenophthis, Osochor, Psinaches and Psusennes. And if this Psusennes is Pasebchanu, and Psinaches is Pinetchem, Osochor is Her-Heru. The other Psusennes is presumably the other Pasebchanu, that is to say, king Aa-cheper-Ra Pasebchanu[e]; and Smendes has perhaps to be identified with king Hetch-cheper-Ra Nesi-Batattat[f], since the town of Batattat was known to

---

[a] Karnak. Mariette, Karnak, plate 41: cf. Mémoires de la Mission Archéologique Française, vol. 1, pp. 694, 695.

[b] See above, page 23 and note e.   [c] See above, page 9 and note d.

[d] See above, page 5 and notes b and c.

[e] Gizeh Museum. Mariette, Monuments divers, plate 102. c.

Gebelain. Recueil de travaux for 1888, vol. 10, p. 135.

the Greeks as Mendes. The last three kings of the Dynasty
having been high priests of Amen in the time of Men-mat-Ra
Rameses and afterwards, their predecessor Amenophthis is
probably the Amen-hetep who was high priest in the time of
Nefer-ka-Ra Rameses[a]. The name Nefer-ka-Ra suggests
Nephercheres: but possibly Nephercheres is intended for
Amen-hetep's father Rameses-Necht, who was high priest in
the time of Heq-mat-Ra Rameses[b].

Manetho assigns this Dynasty to Tanis, while he assigns
Dyn. 20 to Thebes, and makes it consist of twelve kings
whose names he does not state. Very probably, they were
the offspring of the Rameses of Dyns. 18 and 19; though
that is merely a matter of conjecture. But if they were, a
great part of Dyn. 20 must have been concurrent with Dyn.
21, supposing that Osochor is really the high priest Her-Heru
who figures with king Men-mat-Ra Rameses.

In dealing with the kings whom Manetho includes in
Dyn. 21, the book of the Sothis puts kings named Susakim
and Saites in place of Smendes and Osochor, and omits the
second Psusennes. But between Susakim and Thuoris, whom
Manetho places at the end of Dyn. 19, it inserts three kings
named Athothis, Kenkenes and Uennephis, whom Manetho
includes in Dyn. I as the successors of Menes; and it states
that Athothis was also called Psusanos. Standing between the
kings of Dyns. 19 and 21, these three should represent Dyn.
20. But if Psusanos is intended for the second Psusennes,
they ought to come at the end of 21; and such an inversion
is not unlikely in the Sothis, seeing that it puts the kings of
Dyn. 23 before the kings of 22. But, wherever these three
should stand, they cannot represent what Manetho calls Dyn.
20, since he includes them in Dyn. I.

The book of the Sothis allows 98 years for the first six
kings of Dyn. 21, and 28 years for Athothis or Psusanos,
which would raise the total to 126. And the Old Chronicle
limits the Dynasty to six kings in 121 years; whereas
Africanus and Eusebios make it consist of seven kings in 130

---

[a] See below, page 34 and note a.   [b] See below, page 34 and note c.

years, though Africanus fails to account for more than 114 when he enumerates the reigns. Africanus, however, allows 61 years from the accession of Takelothis to the beginning of Dyn. 22, while Eusebios allows 36. And thus, if Takelothis came to the throne in 765[a], Dyn. 21 would have begun in 931 or 940.

Now, various inscriptions can probably be attributed to year 28 of Hetch-cheper-Ra Sheshenk[b], year 16 of User-mat-Ra Amen-em-Apt[c], year 17 of Nutar-cheper-Ra Se-Amen[d] and year 25 of Cha-cheper-Ra Pinetchem[e]; and, if so, these kings must respectively have reigned at least 28, 16, 17 and 25 years. And as User-mat-Ra Sheshenk came to the throne in 790 at latest[f], and these kings seem to have been recognized in succession by the priests at Thebes, Hetch-cheper-Ra Sheshenk would thus have come to the throne in 818 at latest, User-mat-Ra Amen-em-Apt in 834 at latest, Nutar-cheper-Ra Se-Amen in 851 at latest and Cha-cheper-Ra Pinetchem in 876 at latest.

As the high priest Pinetchem seems to have died in year 16 of king User-mat-Ra Amen-em-Apt[c], and Auput was high priest in year 10 of king Hetch-cheper-Ra Sheshenk[h], this Sheshenk must have filled the office of high priest between those dates; always supposing that Auput's father, king Hetch-cheper-Ra Sheshenk, was no other than Pinetchem's nephew Sheshenk, the high priest and king. And if king User-mat-Ra Uasarken was the king Uasarken who married Pinetchem's sister and begot Sheshenk, the probabilities are that Nemart also held the post between those dates ; the high priest Nemart being this Uasarken's son by birth or by adoption[i], and thus a brother of Sheshenk. Nemart may perhaps have been appointed on Pinetchem's death to officiate till Sheshenk came of age ; or even on Sheshenk's accession till Auput came of age. Yet these two pontificates can

---

[a] See above, page 17.
[b] See above, page 24 and note g.
[c] See above, page 25 and note h.
[d] See above, page 26 and note d.
[e] See above, page 27 and note e.
[f] See above, page 12.
[g] See above, page 25 and note h.
[h] See above, page 25 and note e.
[i] See above, page 15.

hardly be compressed into the 9 years that would elapse
between year 16 of User-mat-Ra Amen-em-Apt and year 10
of Hetch-cheper-Ra Sheshenk, if the beginnings of those
reigns are placed in 834 and 818. Perhaps this Uasarken's
reign of 23 years should be interposed between the reigns of
Amen-em-Apt and Sheshenk; or possibly Uasarken succeeded Sheshenk as king, and Nemart succeeded Auput as
high priest, though the pedigrees are rather in favour of the
other view[a]. The previous dates of accession would thus be
carried back 23 years to 857 for Amen-em-Apt, 874 for
Se-Amen, and 899 for Pinetchem.

This Pinetchem has placed his name as king upon the
mummy of king Neb-pehtet-Ra Ahmes[b]; and on several
others he has placed it simply as high priest with dates
extending from year 6 to year 13, and presumably referring
to his predecessor's reign[c]. Her-Heru has also placed his
name upon two mummies as high priest with dates in year 6[d];
and these dates must refer to a previous reign, as one of them
comes later in year 6 than one of those that are mentioned
by Pinetchem, and Pinetchem cannot have become high
priest till Her-Heru resigned. Her-Heru was apparently the
predecessor of Pinetchem on the throne; and as he filled the
office of high priest under Men-mat-Ra Rameses[e], he was
perhaps that king's successor. This Rameses reigned at least
27 years, an inscription being dated in year 27 of his reign[f];
and if the date in year 13 is referred to the reign of Her-
Heru, he must have reigned at least 13 years. And thus,
supposing that Pinetchem came to the throne in 899, Her-
Heru would have come to the throne in 912 at latest, and
Men-mat-Ra Rameses in 939 at latest.

But although Men-mat-Ra Rameses was king at a time

---

[a] See above, pp. 17, 18.   [b] See above, p. 27 and note g.

[c] Gizeh Museum. Maspero, Les momies royales de Déir el-Baharî, in the
Mémoires de la Mission Archéologique Française, vol. 1, pp. 536, 546, 555, 564,
and plate 17. b.

[d] Gizeh Museum. Maspero, ibid., pp. 553, 557, and plates 10. b, 12.

[e] See above, page 23 and note h.

Gizeh Museum. Mariette, Abydos, vol. 2, plate 62. a: cf. Catalogue général
des monuments d'Abydos, no. 1173.

when Her-Heru was merely high priest, Her-Heru may have assumed the rank of king before the death or abdication of this Rameses. In that case Men-mat-Ra need not have come to the throne till 918, if Her-Heru came to the throne in 912 ; since Her-Heru's inscriptions as high priest contain no dates beyond year 6. And as Men-mat-Ra Rameses reigned at least 27 years, and perhaps had Cheper-mat-Ra Rameses for his successor, this line of kings may have survived until the time of Hetch-cheper-Ra Sheshenk, who seems to have called himself a Rameses[a].

Cheper-mat-Ra Rameses reigned at least 3 years, a papyrus being dated in year 3 of his reign[b]: but there is nothing to show for certain whether he came before or after Men-mat-Ra. In all probability, Men-mat-Ra Rameses succeeded Nefer-ka-Ra Rameses. During the reign of Nefer-ka-Ra several of the royal tombs were violated by a gang of thieves; and these robberies led to long investigations. In a papyrus which principally refers to the proceedings in year 16 of king Nefer-ka-Ra, year 19 is described as answering to year 1[c]; and this must mean that Nefer-ka-Ra was then succeeded by another king. A second papyrus refers to the proceedings in year 1[d], and a third refers to those in year 6[e], apparently of this same king, the successor of Nefer-ka-Ra. The papyrus of year 1 states that the thieves had broken into the tombs of kings User-mat-Ra Rameses and Men-mat-Ra Seti. There are endorsements on the coffins of these two kings, stating that they were repaired in year 6 by the high priest Her-Heru[f]. And thus,

---

[a] See above, page 25.
[b] Turin Museum. Champollion, Seconde lettre à M. le Duc de Blacas, plate 13, no. 18.
[c] British Museum. Hawkins, Select papyri in the hieratic character, part 2, plate 8.
[d] Liverpool Museum. Zeitschrift fuer Aegyptische Sprache und Alterthumskunde for 1873, p. 39, for 1874, pp. 61, 62.
[e] Ambras Collection, Vienna. Zeitschrift &c. for 1876, p. 1 and plate 1.
[f] Gizeh Museum. Maspero, Les momies royales de Déir el-Bahari, in the Mémoires de la Mission Archéologique Française, vol. 1, pp. 553, 557, and plates 10. b, 12.

as Her-Heru was high priest under king Men-mat-Ra Rameses, the probabilities are that this Rameses was Nefer-ka-Ra's successor. If so, year 19 of Nefer-ka-Ra was year 1 of Men-mat-Ra; and as Men-mat-Ra came to the throne in 918 at latest, Nefer-ka-Ra would thus have come to the throne in 936 at latest.

Supposing that Osochor, Psinaches and Psusennes, the last three kings of Dyn. 21, may be identified with Her-Heru and his successors Pinetchem and Pasebchanu, who were all high priests as well as kings, Osochor's predecessor Amen-ophthis will presumably be the Amen-hetep who held the office of high priest under king Nefer-ka-Ra Rameses. He is named in a papyrus in year 16 of Nefer-ka-Ra[a], and again in an inscription in year 10, and is described there as a son of the high priest Rameses-necht[b]; while another inscription shows that Rameses-necht was high priest in year 3 of king Heq-mat-Ra Rameses[c].

Heq-mat-Ra reigned 6 years in all; for a papyrus has a list of payments extending from year 2 to year 6 of his reign, and then continuing with years 1, 2 and 3 of the reign after; while the sum total of a salary from his first year to his successor's fourth year is reckoned as ten times the sum for a single year[d]. And thus, if Nefer-ka-Ra came to the throne in 936 at latest, Heq-mat-Ra must have come to the throne in 942 at latest.

Amen-hetep would thus have been high priest from 13 to 19 years after his father, that being the interval between year 3 of Heq-mat-Ra and years 10 and 16 of Nefer-ka-Ra, if Nefer-ka-Ra was Heq-mat-Ra's successor. But here the succession is uncertain.

A bull Apis died in the reign of Nefer-ka-Ra Rameses; and its predecessor seems to have died in the joint reign of

[a] British Museum. Hawkins, Select papyri in the hieratic character, part 2, plate 7.

[b] Karnak. Lepsius, Denkmaeler aus Aegypten, part 3, plate 237. e; cf. Brugsch, Geschichte Aegyptens, p. 632.

[c] Hamamat. Lepsius, ibid., part 3, plate 219. e.

[d] Turin Museum. Zeitschrift fuer Aegyptische Sprache und Alterthumskunde for 1891, pp. 76—78.

Nefer-ka-Ra and Se-cha-en-Ra Rameses, the names of both these kings appearing in its grave[a]. Possibly, Se-cha-en-Ra was succeeded by Nefer-ka-Ra in the interval of seventy days between the death and burial of the sacred animal. His reign, however, must have been ephemeral, as this is the only record of it that remains.

Another Rameses, named User-mat-Ra Se-cheper-en-Ra, seems to have reigned at about the same period with Heq-mat-Ra Rameses; for a couple of inscriptions by the same official, Amen-necht, are dated in year 4 of Heq-mat-Ra and year 4 of Se-cheper-en-Ra[b]. And perhaps Se-cheper-en-Ra was king concurrently with Heq-mat-Ra; being followed on his throne by Se-cha-en-Ra, while Heq-mat-Ra was followed by Nefer-ka-Ra.

The names of both these kings, Se-cheper-en-Ra and Heq-mat-Ra, appear upon the tomb of king Neb-mat-Ra Rameses[c]. Se-cheper-en-Ra's inscriptions are carved upon the entrance; and as they have partly been effaced by Neb-mat-Ra's inscriptions, the probabilities are that Se-cheper-en-Ra began this tomb before the time of Neb-mat-Ra. Heq-mat-Ra's inscriptions are carved in the interior, and may be taken to show that he also had a hand in the construction of the tomb. On an obelisk, however, Neb-mat-Ra's cartouches have been converted into Heq-mat-Ra's[d]; and this looks as though Heq-mat-Ra was reigning after Neb-mat-Ra. The fact may be that these three kings all claimed the throne together; and sometimes one of them, and sometimes another, had the power to enforce his claim.

Neb-mat-Ra Rameses was the second son of the User-mat-Ra Rameses whose epithets were Amen-meri and Heq-Annu, for he occupies the second place in a table of the children of that king[e]. His eldest brother, here styled curtly

---

[a] Mariette, Sérapéum de Memphis, pp. 147, 148, ed. Maspero.
[b] Turin Museum. Recueil de travaux for 1881, vol. 2, pp. 116, 117.
[c] Bab el-Moluk. Lepsius, Denkmaeler aus Aegypten, part 3, plates 223. a, 224. b, c; cf. Mémoires de la Mission Archéologique Française, vol. 3, pp. 48, 78.
[d] Karnak. Champollion, Monuments de l'Égypte, notices, vol. 2, p. 128.
[e] Medinet Habu. Lepsius, ibid., part 3, plate 214. a, c.

Rameses, is doubtless the User-mat-Ra Rameses with the
epithets Setep-en-Amen and Amen-meri Heq-mat, who is
named in a papyrus as the son and successor of the father of
this family[a]. The third son is styled here Rameses At-Amen
Nutar-heq-Annu, and is clearly the king whose name is given
in full upon his tomb as User-mat-Ra Rameses with Amen-
meri Setep-en-Ra and At-Amen Nutar-heq-Annu as epithets[b].
And the fourth son is the User-mat-Ra Rameses whose
epithets were Chu-en-Amen and Amen-meri Seti, his style
and titles being given here in full.

These five kings must all have reigned before the time of
Nefer-ka-Ra Rameses. In an inscription, dated in his reign,
the first three of them are mentioned as deceased, namely,
User-mat-Ra Amen-meri, User-mat-Ra Setep-en-Amen and
Neb-mat-Ra[c]. The tomb of Neb-mat-Ra, the third of them,
is named in a papyrus in connexion with the robberies in his
reign[d]. Rameses Heq-Annu and Rameses At-Amen Nutar-
heq-Annu, the first and fourth of them, seem to have added
their names to an inscription before he added his[e]. And
presumably the fifth of them was not much junior to the
rest.

If they reigned before the time of Nefer-ka-Ra, they must
also have reigned before the time of Se-cha-en-Ra, as he was
practically a contemporary of Nefer-ka-Ra. But their relation to Se-cheper-en-Ra and Heq-mat-Ra can only be a
matter for conjecture; though Neb-mat-Ra, the third of them,
most probably was associated with this pair of kings.

There is nothing to determine the duration of the reigns
of Neb-mat-Ra and his two younger brothers, or that of
Se-cha-en-Ra; and for the reign of Se-cheper-en-Ra there is
nothing but the reference to year 4[f]. For the reign of

[a] British Museum. Birch, Facsimile of an Egyptian hieratic papyrus, plate 79.
[b] Bab el-Moluk. Lepsius, Denkmaeler aus Aegypten, part 3, plate 233.
[c] Abd el-Qurnah. Champollion, Monuments de l'Égypte, notices, vol. 1,
p. 563; cf. Lepsius, ibid., part 3, plate 235.
[d] Liverpool Museum. Zeitschrift fuer Aegyptische Sprache und Alterthumskunde for 1873, p. 40, for 1874, p. 62.
[e] Louvre. Lepsius, Auswahl, plate 14.
[f] See above, page 35 and note b.

User-mat-Ra Rameses Heq-mat there is also a reference to year 4. This occurs in a papyrus[a] without any mention of the king's name; but there is an allusion to the tomb of king User-chau-Ra and a computation that year 3 was four years from year 31, while another papyrus[b] shows that the reign of User-mat-Ra Rameses Heq-mat began in year 32 of king User-mat-Ra Rameses Heq-Annu, the son of king User-chau-Ra Seti-necht.

Allowing 4 years apiece for the reigns of Se-cheper-en-Ra Rameses and User-mat-Ra Rameses Heq-mat, and 32 years for the reign of User-mat-Ra Rameses Heq-Annu, these kings must respectively have come to the throne in 946, 950 and 982 at latest, if Nefer-ka-Ra Rameses and Heq-mat-Ra Rameses came to the throne in 936 and 942 at latest[c]. And then allowing a few years more for the younger brothers of User-mat-Ra Rameses Heq-mat on the supposition that they did not reign concurrently, the accession of king User-mat-Ra Rameses Heq-Annu may roughly be assigned to 1000 at latest.

[a] Mallet Collection. Recueil de travaux for 1880, vol. 1, pp. 47–49.

[b] British Museum. Birch, Facsimile of an Egyptian hieratic papyrus, plates 1, 75, 76, 79.

[c] See above, p. 34.

EGYPTIAN CHRONOLOGY: DYNASTIES XX TO
XVIII AND XII.

In an inscription of king User-mat-Ra Amen-meri Ra-meses Heq-Annu the king is represented with eight of his predecessors on the throne; and the nine monarchs are marshalled in this order:—king User-mat-Ra Amen-meri, king User-chau-Ra Amen-meri, king User-cheperu-Ra Amen-meri, king Ba-en-Ra Amen-meri, king User-mat-Ra Setep-en-Ra, king Men-mat-Ra, king Men-pehtet-Ra, king Ser-cheperu-Ra Setep-en-Ra, and king Neb-mat-Ra[a].

The series is continued in inscriptions of king User-mat-Ra Setep-en-Ra Amen-meri Rameses and king Men-mat-Ra Seti Mer-en-Ptah. These give the names as follows:—king User-mat-Ra Setep-en-Ra, king Men-mat-Ra, king Men-pehtet-Ra, king Ser-cheperu-Ra Setep-en-Ra, king Neb-mat-Ra, king Men-cheperu-Ra, king Aa-cheperu-Ra, king Men-cheper-Ra, king Aa-cheper-en-Ra, king Aa-cheper-ka-Ra, king Ser-ka-Ra, and king Neb-pehtet-Ra[b].

These earlier lists confirm the later list in that portion of the series where they overlap; and in the other portion they are themselves confirmed by evidence of earlier date.

Thus, an officer named Ahmes states in an inscription that he served under king Neb-pehtet-Ra, then under king

---

[a] Medinet Habu. Lepsius, Denkmaeler aus Aegypten, part 3, plate 212.

[b] Ramesseum. Lepsius, ibid., part 3, plates 162, 163. Abydos. Mariette, Abydos, vol. 1, plate 43. British Museum. Mariette, ibid., vol. 2, plate 18.

Ser-ka-Ra, and then under king Aa-cheper-ka-Ra[a]. Another officer of the same name states in more than one inscription that he served under king Neb-pchtet-Ra, then under king Ser-ka-Ra, then under king Aa-cheper-ka-Ra, then under king Aa-cheper-en-Ra, and then under king Men-cheper-Ra[b]. Similarly, an officer named Amen-em-heb states that he served under king Men-cheper-Ra and then under king Aa-cheperu-Ra[c]. An officer named Tchanuni states that he served under king Men-cheper-Ra, then under king Aa-cheperu-Ra, and then under king Men-cheperu-Ra[d]. And an officer named Heru-em-heb states that he served under king Aa-cheperu-Ra, then under king Men-cheperu-Ra, and then under king Neb-mat-Ra[e].

This evidence determines the succession of the kings from Neb-pehtet-Ra to Neb-mat-Ra inclusive; and these eight kings are clearly those whose names appear elsewhere[f] as Neb-pehtet-Ra Ahmes, Ser-ka-Ra Amen-hetep, Aa-cheper-ka-Ra Thothmes, Aa-cheper-en-Ra Thothmes, Men-cheper-Ra Thothmes, Aa-cheperu-Ra Amen-hetep, Men-cheperu-Ra Thothmes, and Neb-mat-Ra Amen-hetep.

The next king in the lists is Ser-cheperu-Ra Setep-en-Ra; and this must be the king whose name is given in full as Ser-cheperu-Ra Heru-em-heb with Setep-en-Ra and Amen-meri as epithets. A block of stone is marked with these cartouches on an erasure of those of king Neb-cheperu-Ra Tut-anch-Amen[g]; and that king describes himself in an inscription as a son of king Neb-mat-Ra Amen-hetep[h]. This seems to show that Tut-anch-Amen reigned between Amen-hetep and

[a] El-Kab. Lepsius, Denkmaeler aus Aegypten, part 3, plate 12. d.

[b] El-Kab. Lepsius, ibid., part 3, plate 43. a. Louvre. Lepsius, Auswahl, plate 14.

[c] Abd el-Qurnah. Zeitschrift fuer Aegyptische Sprache und Alterthumskunde for 1873, p. 7.

[d] Qurnet Murrai. Champollion, Monuments de l'Égypte, notices, vol. 1, pp. 831, 832.

[e] Abd el-Qurnah. Lepsius, Denkmaeler aus Aegypten, part 3, plate 78. a, b. For instance, in the inscriptions published by Lepsius, ibid., part 3, plates 1, 3, 5, 14, 34, 65, 68, 76.

[g] Karnak. Lepsius, ibid., part 3, plate 119. b.

[h] British Museum. Lepsius, Auswahl, plate 13.

Heru-em-heb; and to judge by the position of the graves, a
bull Apis that died in the reign of Tut-anch-Amen must have
been buried after a bull that died in the reign of Amen-hetep
and before two others that died in the reign of Heru-em-heb[a].

Apparently, these all were buried before a bull that died in
the reign of Nefer-cheperu-Ra Chu-en-Aten[b]: yet Chu-en-
Aten's cartouches, as well as those of Tut-anch-Amen and a
king named Ai, are found on stones that Heru-em-heb employed for buildings of his own at Thebes[c]. And this looks
as though Heru-em-heb followed Chu-en-Aten on the throne
at Thebes, though possibly at Memphis the order was
reversed.

This king Nefer-cheperu-Ra Chu-en-Aten can only be
king Nefer-cheperu-Ra Amen-hetep under another name, his
person being represented with all the characteristics of Chu-
en-Aten in reliefs in which his name is given as Amen-hetep[d].
And no doubt he changed his name on adopting the worship
of the Aten in place of that of Amen. He certainly was
junior to Neb-mat-Ra Amen-hetep, for he is represented in
adoration of that king[e]. And possibly he was a son-in-law ;
Neb-mat-Ra being described as the husband of a queen
named Thii[f], while a queen named Thii is described as the
mother of the queen in Chu-en-Aten's reign[g].

A king Anch-cheperu-Ra Se-aa-ka-Ra must also have
reigned about this time, the inscriptions showing that his
queen was called Aten-meri-ta[h]—a name that was borne by
one of Chu-en-Aten's daughters[i], and not likely to remain in
use after the worship of the Aten had collapsed. Very probably king Cheper-cheperu-Ra Ai also reigned about this time,

[a] Mariette, Sérapéum de Memphis, pp. 124—131, ed. Maspero.

[b] Mariette, ibid., pp. 131—137 ; part 3, plate 6.

[c] Recueil de travaux for 1885, vol. 6, p. 54.

[d] Abd el-Qurnah. Villiers Stuart, The funeral tent of an Egyptian queen,
pp. 89 ff.

[e] Soleb. Lepsius, Denkmaeler aus Aegypten, part 3, plate 110. k.

[f] Sedinga. Lepsius, ibid., part 3, plate 82. f—i.

[g] Tell el-Amarna. Lepsius, ibid., part 3, plate 100. c.

[h] Tell el-Amarna. Lepsius, ibid., part 3, plate 99. a.

[i] Tell el-Amarna. Lepsius, ibid., part 3, plate 103.

as stones of his are mixed with stones of Chu-en-Aten's and Tut-anch-Amen's in Heru-em-heb's buildings[a]. But, although he styles himself a priest in his cartouches, he cannot safely be identified with either of the priests named Ai who held high office under Chu-en-Aten. They built themselves tombs in Chu-en-Aten's city[b]; and he was buried in the tomb he built at Thebes[c].

According to his own account, Heru-em-heb was placed upon the throne at Thebes by the intervention of the gods[d]; and this may be taken to show that he had not any legal right there. But as he claims descent from Men-cheper-Ra[e], the fourth king before him in the lists, he was probably some cousin of the Neb-mat-Ra who was reckoned as his predecessor.

The two next kings in the lists, Men-pehtet-Ra and Men-mat-Ra, must be kings Men-pehtet-Ra Rameses and Men-mat-Ra Seti Mer-en-Ptah. An inscription shows that this Rameses was the father of this Seti[f]; and another seems to show that both these kings were reigning at one time[g]. The next king is clearly the User-mat-Ra Rameses whose epithets were Setep-en-Ra and Amen-meri. He appears in an inscription as a son of king Men-mat-Ra Seti Mer-en-Ptah[h]; and the lists themselves give both these names in full[i]. Moreover, an inscription seems to show that these two kings were also reigning at one time[j]. The next king, Ba-en-Ra Amen-meri, is presumably the Mer-en-Ptah who is distinguished by the royal cartouche as Ba-en-Ra Nuteru-meri in a table of the children of this Rameses[k]. Elsewhere his name

[a] See above, page 40 and note c.

[b] Tell el-Amarna. Lepsius, Denkmaeler aus Aegypten, part 3, plates 103—106. a, 107. d—109.

[c] Bab el-Moluk. Lepsius, ibid., part 3, plate 113.

[d] Turin Museum. Transactions of the Society of Biblical Archaeology, vol. 3, pp. 486 ff. and plates thereto.

[e] Der el-Bahari. Lepsius, ibid., part 3, plate 119. c.

[f] Qurnah. Lepsius, ibid., part 3, plate 131. b.

[g] Karnak. Lepsius, ibid., part 3, plate 124. b.

[h] Abydos. Mariette, Abydos, vol. 1, plates 5—9.

See above, page 38.   [j] Qurnah. Lepsius, ibid., part 3, plate 132. f.

[k] Ramesseum. Lepsius, ibid., part 3, plate 168.

is given in full as Ba-en-Ra Mer-en-Ptah with Amen-meri
and Hetep-her-mat as epithets[a].

Thus the succession was continuous in these four generations. But a king Chu-en-Ra Setep-en-Ra Mer-en-Ptah
Se-Ptah is represented in adoration of two of these kings,
Men-mat-Ra and User-mat-Ra Setep-en-Ra[b]: and this shows
that he reigned after them. Yet the tomb of his queen,
Ta-user-ta, has been appropriated first by User-cheperu-Ra
Amen-meri and then by User-chau-Ra Amen-meri[c]; so that
he must have reigned before those kings, although the list has
got them next to Ba-en-Ra.

The name of User-chau-Ra is given here in full as
User-chau-Ra Seti-necht with Setep-en-Ra Amen-meri and
Ra-meri Amen-meri as epithets; and an inscription seems
to show that he was reigning at the same time with the
User-mat-Ra Rameses whose epithets were Amen-meri and
Heq-Annu[d]. According to a papyrus of that period, he was
the father of this Rameses; and had been placed upon the
throne by the intervention of the gods when Egypt was lost
in anarchy[e].

The list shows that this Rameses regarded User-cheperu-
Ra Amen-meri as his father's predecessor; and that king's
name appears elsewhere as User-cheperu-Ra Amen-meri Seti
Mer-en-Ptah[f]. But this Rameses and his father must have
reigned after a king Men-mat-Ra Amen-meses; for they had
to give their tomb an awkward angle in order to keep it clear
of his[g]. Yet an inscription shows that he reigned after
Men-mat-Ra Seti Mer-en-Ptah[h]. And as that king was
succeeded by his son and grandson, Men-mat-Ra Amen-

[a] Surarieh. Lepsius, Denkmaeler aus Aegypten, part 3, plate 198.

[b] Qurnah. Lepsius, ibid., part 3, plate 201. c.

[c] Bab el-Moluk. Champollion, Monuments de l'Égypte, notices, vol. 1,
pp. 448—451.

[d] Medinet Habu. Lepsius, ibid., part 3, plate 206. d.

[e] British Museum. Birch, Facsimile of an Egyptian hieratic papyrus, plates
75, 76; cf. 1.

[f] Abu Simbel. Lepsius, ibid., part 3, plate 204. e.

[g] Bab el-Moluk. Mémoires de la Mission Archéologique Française, vol. 3,
p. 84.

[h] Medinet Habu. Lepsius ibid., part 3, plate 202. d.

meses may be placed with Chu-en-Ra about the time of
User-cheperu-Ra Seti Mer-en-Ptah.

Thus the lists would seem to be defective here, and also in
the time of Ser-cheperu-Ra Heru-em-heb, as they ignore two
groups of kings. Most probably, however, they give the
succession that was regarded as legitimate; tacitly assuming
that Heru-em-heb came to the throne by right, if not in fact,
immediately upon the death of Neb-mat-Ra Amen-hetep;
and making similar assumptions about the first Rameses, the
second Seti, and also Seti-necht.

Now, supposing that User-mat-Ra Rameses Heq-Annu
came to the throne in 1000 at latest[a], and that the lists
enumerate his fifteen predecessors in their proper order, an
epoch may be found for all these kings.

A papyrus is dated in year 1 of king User-chau-Ra Seti-
necht[b], so that he reigned at least 1 year by himself. An
inscription is dated in year 2 of king User-cheperu-Ra Seti
Mer-en-Ptah[c], so that he reigned at least 2 years. And an
inscription is dated in year 25 or 33 of king Ba-en-Ra Mer-
en-Ptah[d], so that he reigned at least 25 or 33 years; the
question being whether two strokes are the remains of two
units or a ten. As for the other kings belonging to this
period, an inscription is dated in year 3 of king Chu-en-Ra
Mer-en-Ptah Se-Ptah[e], so that he reigned at least 3 years:
but nothing has been discovered with a date in the reign
of king Men-mat-Ra Amen-meses. Excluding these two
kings from the succession, and taking the lower date for the
reign of Ba-en-Ra Mer-en-Ptah, his accession may thus be
placed in 1028 at latest.

The great User-mat-Ra Rameses, whose epithets were
Setep-en-Ra and Amen-meri, reigned for 67 years; the fact
being mentioned by king Heq-mat-Ra Rameses in one of his

---

[a] See above, page 37.
[b] British Museum. Hawkins, Select papyri in the hieratic character: Sallier
papyrus no. 1, plate 6 verso.
[c] Silseleh. Champollion, Monuments de l'Égypte, notices, vol. 1, p. 258.
[d] Karnak. Brugsch, Reiseberichte aus Aegypten, p. 194.
[e] Sehel. Lepsius, Denkmaeler aus Aegypten, part 3, plate 202. b.

inscriptions[a]. This reign would thus have lasted from 1095 to 1028 at latest.

Inscriptions are dated in year 9 of king Men-mat-Ra Seti Mer-en-Ptah[b], so that he reigned at least 9 years, coming to the throne in 1104 at latest. An inscription is dated in year 2 of king Men-pehtet-Ra Rameses[c], so that he reigned at least 2 years, coming to the throne in 1106 at latest. An inscription is dated in year 21 of king Ser-cheperu-Ra Heru-em-heb[d], so that he reigned at least 21 years, coming to the throne in 1127 at latest. And an inscription is dated in year 36 of king Neb-mat-Ra Amen-hetep[e], so that he reigned at least 36 years, coming to the throne in 1163 at latest.

As for the other kings belonging to this period, an inscription is dated in year 12 of king Nefer-cheperu-Ra Chu-en-Aten[f], so that he reigned at least 12 years; and an inscription is dated in year 4 of king Cheper-cheperu-Ra Ai[g], so that he reigned at least 4 years: but nothing has come to light with dates of king Neb-cheperu-Ra Tut-anch-Amen or king Anch-cheperu-Ra Se-aa-ka-Ra. These four kings must all have reigned after king Neb-mat-Ra Amen-hetep[h]. Yet the probabilities are that their reigns should not be reckoned independently, but should rather be included in the reign of Ser-cheperu-Ra Heru-em-heb. And as Tut-anch-Amen was Amen-hetep's son[i], his accession may thus be placed in 1127 at latest.

An inscription is dated in year 7 of king Men-cheperu-Ra Thothmes[j], so that he reigned at least 7 years, coming to the throne in 1170 at latest. An inscription is dated in year 5 of

[a] Abydos. Mariette, Abydos, vol. 2, plates 34, 35.

[b] Redesieh and Assuan. Lepsius, Denkmaeler aus Aegypten, part 3, plates 140. b, 141. i.

[c] Louvre. Champollion, Monuments de l'Égypte, vol. 1, plate 1, no. 2.

[d] British Museum. Zeitschrift fuer Aegyptische Sprache und Alterthumskunde for 1876, pp. 122, 123.

[e] Sarbut el-Chadem. Lepsius, ibid., part 3, plate 71. c, d.

[f] Tell el-Amarna. Lepsius, ibid., part 3, plate 100. b.

[g] Berlin Museum. Lepsius, ibid., part 3, plate 114. i.

[h] See above, pp. 39, 40.　　　[i] See above, page 39 and note h.
Konosso. Lepsius, ibid., part 3, plate 69. e.

king Aa-cheperu-Ra Amen-hetep[a], so that he reigned at least
5 years, coming to the throne in 1175 at latest. And an inscription of this period shows that Men-cheper-Ra Thothmes
reigned for 54 years[b], so that he must have come to the
throne in 1229 at latest.

Finally, an inscription is dated in year 1 of king Aa-
cheper-en-Ra Thothmes[c], so that he reigned at least 1 year,
coming to the throne in 1230 at latest. An inscription is
dated in year 9 of king Aa-cheper-ka-Ra Thothmes[d], so that
he reigned at least 9 years, coming to the throne in 1239 at
latest. An inscription is dated in year 10 of king Ser-ka-Ra
Amen-hetep[e], so that he reigned at least 10 years, coming to
the throne in 1249 at latest. And an inscription is dated in
year 22 of king Neb-pehtet-Ra Ahmes[f], so that he reigned
at least 22 years, coming to the throne in 1271 at latest.

An officer named Ahmes, who states in an inscription that
he served under this Neb-pehtet-Ra and the two next kings,
states also that his father served under Se-qenen-Ra[g]. And
this is presumably the king Se-qenen-Ra Tau-aaqen whose
mummy was found with those of king Neb-pehtet-Ra Ahmes
and his successors[h]. To judge by the aspect of the mummy,
Se-qenen-Ra was killed in battle; and a papyrus indicates
the outbreak of a quarrel between a king Se-qenen-Ra in the
valley of the Nile and a king Apepi in the Delta[i], while the
inscription of Ahmes[g] speaks of the conquest of the Delta by
king Neb-pehtet-Ra Ahmes at the beginning of his reign.

This war seems to mark the boundary between Dyns. 17
and 18. The two main versions of Manetho agree that

[a] Bibliothèque Nationale, Paris. Pleyte, Les papyrus Rollin, plate 15.

[b] Abd el-Qurnah. Zeitschrift fuer Aegyptische Sprache und Alterthumskunde
for 1873, p. 7.

[c] Assuan. Lepsius, Denkmaeler aus Aegypten, part 3, plate 16. a.

[d] Karnak. Mariette, Karnak, plate 32. f.

[e] Gizeh Museum. Recueil de travaux for 1887, vol. 9, p. 94.

[f] Masarah. Lepsius, ibid., part 3, plate 3. a, b.

[g] El-Kab. Lepsius, ibid., part 3, plate 12. d.

[h] Gizeh Museum. Maspero, Les momies royales de Déir el-Bahari, in the
Mémoires de la Mission Archéologique Française, vol. 1, p. 526, and plate 3.

[i] British Museum. Hawkins, Select papyri in the hieratic character: Sallier
papyrus no. 1, plates 1—3.

Dyn. 18 began with a king Amosis, who answers to Neb-pehtet-Ra Ahmes. The version in Eusebios makes Dyn. 17 consist of shepherd kings, and gives the name of one of them as Aphophis, which is certainly a variant of Apepi. The version in Africanus makes the shepherd kings of Dyn. 17 concurrent with a line of kings at Thebes ; and apparently Se-qenen-Ra was king at Thebes, while Apepi was reigning in the Delta. And both these versions say that the shepherd kings held Memphis[a].

The succession is clear from Neb-pehtet-Ra Ahmes to Men-cheperu-Ra Thothmes and Neb-mat-Ra Amen-hetep, the sixth and seventh kings after him[b]; and these must be the kings Tuthmosis and Amenophis whom Manetho places sixth and seventh after Amosis in his list of Dyn. 18. The next name, Oros, may be intended for Ser-cheperu-Ra Heru-em-heb. But between Amosis and Tuthmosis there are Chebros, Amenophthis, Amensis, Misaphris and Misphrag-muthosis ; and their names can hardly be adapted to the kings who reigned between Neb-pehtet-Ra Ahmes and Men-cheperu-Ra Thothmes. Next after Oros come Acherres, Rathos, Chebres, Acherres, Cherres and Armesses. This is the point at which the legitimate succession seems to have been broken by the reigns of Tut-anch-Amen, Chu-en-Aten, Se-aa-ka-Ra and Ai[c]; but here again the names can scarcely be identified. Then come Ramesses and Amenophthis, ending Dyn. 18 ; and then Sethos, Rampsakes, Ammeneph-thes, Ramesses, Ammenemnes and Thuoris, forming Dyn. 19. Ramesses, Sethos and Rampsakes may answer to the next three kings in the legitimate succession, namely, Men-pehtet-Ra Rameses, Men-mat-Ra Seti and User-mat-Ra Rameses[d] ; and possibly Ammenemnes and Thuoris may answer to Men-mat-Ra Amen-meses and queen Ta-user-ta, who reigned just afterwards[e]. But there is still a difficulty in identifying the Amenophthis at the end of Dyn. 18, and the Ammeneph-

---

[a] Syncellos, p. 61, δυναστεία ποιμένων...Φοίνικες ξένοι βασιλεῖς, οἳ καὶ Μέμφιν εἷλον.

[b] See above, page 39.

[c] See above, page 40.

[d] See above, page 41.

[e] See above, page 42.

thes and Ramesses of Dyn. 19; and also in perceiving why the accession of Sethos should produce a change of Dynasty. The two main versions of Manetho assign Dyns. 18 and 19 to Thebes, and so also Dyn. 20, and then assign Dyn. 21 to Tanis. They do not specify the names of any of the kings in 20; but as the second name in 19 seems to be intended for the great User-mat-Ra Rameses, and the fifth name in 21 for a contemporary of Men-mat-Ra Rameses[a], the presumption is that Dyn. 20 consisted of the intervening kings who bore the name of Rameses. The first four names in 21 would thus belong to kings who reigned concurrently with those of 20, or even of 19; and possibly they were connected with an earlier Dynasty, since the Old Chronicle assigns 16 to Tanis as well as 21. This assigns 17 and 18 to Memphis, and only 19 and 20 to Thebes; but here the versions are at variance, Dyn. 17 in Eusebios answering to Dyn. 15 in Africanus. Both these versions make this Dynasty consist of shepherd kings at Memphis; but Africanus continues the shepherd kings in Dyns. 16 and 17, only making those of 17 concurrent with a Dynasty of kings at Thebes, whereas Eusebios introduces Thebes for 15 and 16. They agree, however, in assigning Dyn. 14 to Xois and Dyn. 13 to Thebes; but in all these Dynasties, except 15 or 17, they omit to state the names of any of the kings. Africanus gives the names in Dyn. 15 as Saites, Bnon, Pachnan, Staan, Archles and Aphobis; and these are substantially the names in Dyn. 17 of Eusebios and the Sothis, and also those of the shepherd kings, as given by Josephus[b]. But there is little prospect of identifying any of these names, excepting Aphobis or Aphophis, which must be Apepi.

Africanus and Eusebios both assign Dyns. 11 and 12 to Thebes, putting king Ammenemes between the two, and making 12 consist of Sesonchosis, Ammanemes, Sesostris, Lachares, Ameres, Amenemes and Skemiophris, a queen. And these names seem to be intended for king Se-hetep-ab-Ra Amen-em-ha, king Cheper-ka-Ra Usertesen, king

---

[a] See above, pp. 29, 30.　　　[b] Josephus, contra Apionem, i. 14.

Nub-kau-Ra Amen-em-ha, king Cha-cheper-Ra Usertesen, king Cha-kau-Ra Usertesen, king Mat-en-Ra Amen-em-ha, king Mat-cheru-Ra Amen-em-ha and queen Sebek-em-sas.

The true succession can be traced as far as king Neb-pehtet-Ra Ahmes by means of the lists in the inscriptions[a]. But one of these lists has only Neb-cheru-Ra and Mena before Neb-pehtet-Ra[b], while another has eight kings between Neb-pehtet-Ra and Neb-cheru-Ra, and fifty-five between Neb-cheru-Ra and Mena[c]. The eight are king Mat-cheru-Ra, king Mat-en-Ra, king Cha-kau-Ra, king Cha-cheper-Ra, king Nub-kau-Ra, king Cheper-ka-Ra, king Se-hetep-ab-Ra, and king Se-anch-ka-Ra. Another list, however, reverses the order of this group, putting king Neb-cheru-Ra next to king Neb-pehtet-Ra, and ascending thence to king Mat-cheru-Ra[d]. But this is clearly a mistake, the order being fixed by an inscription which enumerates the dignities conferred upon a man's maternal grandfather by king Se-hetep-ab-Ra Amen-em-ha and afterwards by king Cheper-ka-Ra Usertesen, upon the man himself by king Nub-kau-Ra Amen-em-ha, and upon his eldest son by king Cha-cheper-Ra Usertesen[e]. The next three kings in the list, Cha-kau-Ra, Mat-en-Ra and Mat-cheru-Ra, presumably are those whose names are given elsewhere in full as Cha-kau-Ra Usertesen, Mat-en-Ra Amen-em-ha and Mat-cheru-Ra Amen-em-ha[f]. And as Africanus calls Skemiophris a sister of Amenemes, or Mat-cheru-Ra Amen-em-ha, she is perhaps the queen Sebek-em-sas who is styled a royal sister and royal wife in an inscription which associates her with queen Ah-hetep, the mother of king Neb-pehtet-Ra Ahmes[g].

In placing king Mat-cheru-Ra next to king Neb-pehtet-Ra, the list brings Dyn. 18 into contact with Dyn. 12. Yet

---

[a] See above, page 38.

[b] Ramesseum. Lepsius, Denkmaeler aus Aegypten, part 3, plate 163.

[c] Abydos. Mariette, Abydos, vol. 1, plate 43.

[d] Gizeh Museum. Mariette, Monuments divers, plate 58.

[e] Beni Hassan. Lepsius, ibid., part 2, plates 124, 125.

[f] For instance, in the inscriptions published by Lepsius, ibid., part 2, plates 135, 138, and Koenigsbuch, no. 184.

[g] Gizeh Museum. Recueil de travaux for 1887, vol. 9, p. 93.

there was certainly a break in the succession here, as Neb-pehtet-Ra was preceded by Se-qenen-Ra and Apepi[a]. The list may have omitted these two kings, and possibly some others of that period, just as it omits two groups of kings about the time of Heru-em-Heb and Seti-necht[b], presumably upon the ground that they were illegitimate. But the list could hardly have ignored the kings before Neb-pehtet-Ra, had they constituted five entire Dynasties.

In another list in a papyrus[c] king Mat-cheru-Ra is followed by a king Sebek-neferu-Ra and then (if the fragments have been joined aright) by a number of kings who cannot be included in Dyn. 18 or any later Dynasty, and therefore have to be assigned to Dyns. 13 to 17. But many of these kings appear again in an inscription[d] of king Men-cheper-Ra Thothmes which represents a series of his ancestors in double file ; and here these kings are ranged upon the right, while Se-qenen-Ra and Sebek-neferu-Ra and Mat-cheru-Ra and his predecessors in Dyn. 12 are ranged upon the left. And this arrangement seems to show that these kings of Dyns. 13 to 17 could not have reigned between Dyn. 12 and Dyn. 18, but must have formed a separate monarchy in some outlying part of Egypt, while those Dynasties held Thebes.

Besides these kings who have to be assigned to Dyns. 13 to 17, there clearly were some others, such as Se-qenen-Ra's opponent Apepi or Aphophis, whom Manetho includes among the shepherd kings. Josephus quotes Manetho as saying that the shepherd kings were known in Egypt as the Hyksos; and he derives the name from Hyk, a king, and Sos, a shepherd[e]. But probably the name was Heq-Shas or Hequ-Shasu, which would denote the kings or princes of the Shas or Shasu[f], a tribe that lived beyond the north-east boundary of Egypt. And Africanus and Eusebios both quote Manetho as saying that these shepherd kings were foreigners from

[a] See above, page 45.   [b] See above, pp. 39—41 and 42, 43.
[c] Turin Museum. Lepsius, Auswahl, plate 5, col. 7.
[d] Bibliothèque Nationale, Paris. Lepsius, ibid., plate 1.
[e] Josephus, contra Apionem, i. 14.
[f] Karnak. Lepsius, Denkmaeler aus Aegypten, part 3, plate 128.

T.   4

Phœnicia[a]. So the regular succession may have been disturbed by intruders from abroad as well as rival claimants in the country. Yet there is nothing to indicate that any great length of time elapsed between Dyn. 12 and Dyn. 18.

But even if Mat-cheru-Ra had actually come next before Neb-pehtet-Ra, there would still be a difficulty in settling dates within Dyn. 12. An inscription shows that year 30 of king Se-hetep-ab-Ra Amen-em-ha was year 10 of king Cheper-ka-Ra Usertesen[b]; so that Se-hetep-ab-Ra reigned only 20 years apart from Cheper-ka-Ra. Another inscription shows that year 44 of king Cheper-ka-Ra Usertesen was year 2 of king Nub-kau-Ra Amen-em-ha[c]; so that Cheper-ka-Ra reigned only 42 years apart from Nub-kau-Ra. And another inscription shows that year 35 of king Nub-kau-Ra Amen-em-ha was year 3 of king Cha-cheper-Ra Usertesen[d]; so that Nub-kau-Ra reigned only 32 years apart from Cha-Cheper-Ra. This king Cha-cheper-Ra Usertesen reigned at least 7 years, an inscription being dated in year 7 of his reign[e]; but this is not a proof that he was reigning by himself so late as year 7, for an inscription is dated in year 29 of king Se-hetep-ab-Ra Amen-em-ha[f], although that king ceased to reign by himself after year 20. In the same way, Cha-kau-Ra Usertesen reigned at least 19 years, an inscription being dated in year 19 of his reign[g]; Mat-en-Ra Amen-em-ha reigned at least 44 years, an inscription being dated in year 44 of his reign[h]; and Mat-cheru-Ra Amen-em-ha reigned at least 5 years, an inscription being dated in year 5 of his reign[i]. But other

---

[a] Syncellos, p. 61, ἦσαν δὲ Φοίνικες ξένοι.

[b] Gizeh Museum. Mariette, Catalogue général des monuments d'Abydos, no. 558.

[c] Leyden Museum. Lepsius, Auswahl, plate 10.

[d] Assuan. Lepsius, ibid., plate 10, and Denkmaeler aus Aegypten, part 2, plate 123. e.   [e] British Museum. No. 575.

[f] Korosko. Zeitschrift fuer Aegyptische Sprache und Alterthumskunde for 1882, p. 30.

[g] Geneva Museum. Mélanges d'archéologie Égyptienne et Assyrienne for 1873, vol. 1, p. 218.

[h] Sarbut el-Chadem. Champollion, Monuments de l'Égypte, notices, vol. 2, p. 691.

[i] Berlin Museum. Lepsius, Denkmaeler aus Aegypten, part 2, plate 152. f.

inscriptions seem to show that Cha-kau-Ra reigned with Mat-en-Ra[a], and that Mat-en-Ra reigned with Mat-cheru-Ra[b]; so that a great part of the 44 years of Mat-en-Ra may have been included in the 19 years of Cha-kau-Ra and the 5 years of Mat-cheru-Ra. And thus the real duration of the reigns cannot be determined.

Supposing, however, that Neb-pehtet-Ra Ahmes came to the throne in 1271 at latest[c]; that Mat-cheru-Ra reigned next before; and that there was not any overlapping of the reigns of Mat-cheru-Ra, Mat-en-Ra, Cha-kau-Ra and Cha-cheper-Ra, these inscriptions would yield the following results:—Mat-cheru-Ra Amen-em-ha must have come to the throne in 1276 at latest, Mat-en-Ra Amen-em-ha in 1320 at latest, Cha-kau-Ra Usertesen in 1339 at latest, Cha-cheper-Ra Usertesen in 1346 at latest, Nub-kau-Ra Amen-em-ha in 1378 at latest, Cheper-ka-Ra Usertesen in 1420 at latest, and Se-hetep-ab-Ra Amen-em-ha in 1440 at latest. And then allowing for a gap between Mat-cheru-Ra Amen-em-ha and Neb-pehtet-Ra Ahmes, the beginning of Dyn. 12 might thus be placed about 1500 at latest.

In an inscription of the time of king User-mat-Ra Setep-en-Ra Amen-meri Rameses there is a date in year 400 of king Aa-pehtet-Set Nubti-Set[d]. If the date is accurate, and Nubti really was a king and not a deity, he must have come to the throne between 1495 and 1428 at latest, this Rameses having reigned from 1095 to 1028 at latest[e]. But there is nothing to fix the place of Nubti among the kings of Egypt.

The story of the Exodus is useless for determining dates. In speaking of the sojourn of the Jews in Egypt, the Bible does not mention any king by name. And this omission, coupled with the silence of the monuments as to any such occurrence as the Exodus, seems to show that the story must

[a] Gizeh Museum. Mariette, Abydos, vol. 2, plates 24, 25.
[b] Berlin Museum. Lepsius, Denkmaeler aus Aegypten, part 2, plate 140. m. Louvre. Lepsius, Auswahl, plate 10.
[c] See above, page 45.
[d] Tanis. Revue Archéologique for 1865, vol. 11, plate 4.
[e] See above, pp. 43, 44.

be treated as a parable that has no base in history. But even if the Pharaohs of the Bible were to be identified, this evidence would scarcely serve to fix their dates; the computation of the various periods being so confused and contradictory that the numerals appear to be corrupt.

The invasion of Shishak in year 5 of Rehoboam is placed 41 years after the founding of the Temple in year 4 of Solomon, that king's reign being reckoned as 40 years[a]. And the founding of the Temple is placed 480 years after the Exodus[b]. Yet no less than 533 years are allotted to events between the Exodus and the founding of the Temple, besides the years required for the government of Joshua and the elders, of Shamgar, and of Saul[c]. And even if the Exodus could actually be placed 521 years before the invasion of Shishak, no definite result would be obtained, the date of that invasion being so uncertain[d].

---

[a] Chronicles, ii. 3. 2, 9. 30, 12. 2; Kings, i. 6. 1, 11. 42, 14. 25.

[b] Kings, i. 6. 1.

[c] Deuteronomy, i. 3; Judges, 3. 8, 11, 14, 30, 31, 4. 3, 5. 31, 6. 1, 8. 28, 9. 22, 10. 2, 3, 8, 12. 7, 9, 11, 14, 13. 1, 16. 31; Samuel, i. 4. 18; Kings, i. 2. 11, 6. 1.

[d] See above, pp. 19-21.

IV.

EGYPTIAN CHRONOLOGY: THE CALENDAR, ETC.

A phœnix appeared in Egypt in 34 or 36 A.D.[a]. According to Tacitus, its three predecessors had appeared there in the reigns of Ptolemy III, Amasis and Sesosis[b]. Thus, if these birds appeared at regular intervals, their period could not be more than 282 years, that being the time between 36 A.D. and the accession of this Ptolemy in 247 B.C.; nor could it be less than 279 years, that being the time between 247 B.C. and the death of Amasis in 526 B.C. Taking the period as 280 years, and placing these birds at 34 A.D. and 247 and 527 B.C., their predecessor must be placed at 807 B.C. And as this date seems to fall in the reign of Sesonchis[c], he is possibly the king that Tacitus calls Sesosis.

Tacitus remarks that the period was generally supposed to be 500 years, though some said 1461; but neither version could be reconciled with history. The period is reckoned as 500 years by most of the Greek and Latin authors, beginning with Herodotos[d]: but some of them give other computations.

[a] Pliny, x. 2, Solinus, 33, and Dion Cassius, lviii. 27, give 36 A.D., while Tacitus, annales, vi. 28, gives 34 A.D. According to Pliny and Solinus, the bird was brought to Rome in 47 A.D.; and Aurelius Victor, de Cæsaribus, 4, and Dexippos, apud Syncellum, p. 334, seem to have confounded its arrival in Rome with its appearance in Egypt.

[b] Tacitus, annales, vi. 28.   [c] See above, pp. 16–18.

[d] Herodotos, ii. 73; Ælian, de natura animalium, vi. 58; Philostratos, vita Apollonii, iii. 49; Horapollon, hieroglyphica, i. 35; Mela, chorographia, iii. 8; Seneca, epistolæ, 42; Ovid, metamorphoses, xv. 395; Clemens Romanus, ad Corinthios, i. 25; Cyrillus Hierosolymitanus, catecheses, 18. 8; Epiphanios, ancoratus, 84, physiologus, 11; etc.

Pliny and Solinus make it 540 years[a]; and Solinus says
that others made it 12,954. Dexippos makes it 654 years[b].
Hesiod seems to have made it 972 years, or some multiple
of that[c]. Chæremon makes it 7006 years[d]. And several
authors make it 1000 years[e]. But these statements are useless for determining dates, as there is nothing in them to
connect the former appearances of the phœnix with any
events on record.

Censorinus and Chalcidius associate the period of 1461
years with the dog-star, Sirius or Sothis[f]; and Censorinus
says that the period began when the dog-star rose on day 1
of month 1. Supposing that it rose at intervals of exactly
365¼ days while the year had only 365, the rising would fall
a quarter of a day later every year ; and thus would eventually
come round again to day 1 of month 1 after the lapse of
four times 365¼ years, or 1461 years of 365 days each.

In the Canopic decree of 238 B.C. the rising of the dog-
star is placed on day 1 of month 10[g]. And as there were
thirty days in each month with five odd days at the end of
the year, day 1 of month 10 was 95 days from day 1 of
month 1 in the year after. Now, if the dog-star rose a
quarter of a day later every year, it would rise 95 days later
after the lapse of four times 95 years ; and thus would rise
on day 1 of month 1 in 143 A.D. And an Alexandrian coin[h] of
143 A.D. has the figure of a phœnix with the legend ΑΙΩΝ.

[a] Pliny, x. 2; Solinus, 33.   [b] Dexippos, apud Syncellum, p. 334.

[c] Plutarch, de defectu oraculorum, 11 ; Ausonius, idyllia, 18. 3-6; Pliny, vii.
49. According to these authors, Hesiod made a phœnix live nine times as long
as a raven, a raven three times as long as a stag, a stag four times as long as a
crow, and a crow nine times as long as a man. Plutarch says that some
understood a man's life to mean a year, others 30 years, and others 108. Ausonius
makes it 96.

[d] Chæremon, apud Tzetzen, chiliades, v. 397.

[e] Martial, epigrammata, v. 7; Claudian, idyllia, i. 27; Lactantius, de phœnice,
59; Nonnos, dionysiaca, xl. 395.

[f] Censorinus, de die natali, 18 ; Chalcidius, in Timæum, 125.

[g] Gizeh Museum. Lepsius, Das bilingue Dekret von Kanopus, plate 3, line 18,
and plate 6, lines 36, 37.

[h] British Museum. Catalogue of Greek coins, Alexandria, no. 1004. The date
is year 6 of Antoninus Pius.

This phœnix, however, may indicate a period of 500 years which terminated then. In the Egyptian calendar the months were reckoned as three tetramens, or groups of four months each, day 1 of month 9 being counted as day 1 of month 1 in tetramen 3. Thus, if the dog-star rose in 143 A.D. at the beginning of the first tetramen, it would have risen at the beginning of the third tetramen 500 years before; day 1 of month 9 being 125 days from day 1 of month 1 in the ensuing year. And this might be regarded as a transition from new-year to new-year, since the Greeks and Romans took these tetramens for years[a].

Writing in 238 A.D., Censorinus calculates that 139 A.D. must have been the year in which the dog-star rose on day 1 of month 1[b]; and apparently Clement of Alexandria also reckoned from that date.

Clement places the Exodus of the Jews in the time of Inachos of Argos, 345 years before the Sothic period. He computes four generations from the Exodus to the deluge of Deucalion in the time of Crotopos of Argos; then 73 years to the conflagration on mount Ida and the discovery of iron by the Dactyls; 65 years to the rape of Ganymede; 15 years to the institution of the Isthmian games; 34 years to the foundation of Troy; 64 years to the voyage of the Argo; 32 years to the contest of Theseus with the Minotaur; 10 years to the war of the seven against Thebes; 3 years to the institution of the Olympic games; 9 years to the campaign of the Amazons against the Athenians; 11 years to the death of Heracles; and 4 years to the rape of Helen: then 10 years from the fall of Troy to the founding of Lavinium by Æneas; 8 years to the reign of Ascanius; 61 years to the return of the Heracleidæ; and 338 years to the Olympiad of Iphitos[c].

He thus accounts for 737 years; to which 20 must be added for the interval between the rape of Helen and the

[a] Plutarch, vita Numæ, 18; Censorinus, de die natali, 19; Augustinus, de civitate Dei, xv. 12.
[b] Censorinus, de die natali, 21.
[c] Clemens Alexandrinus, stromateis, i. 21. 136, 137.

fall of Troy[a], and 134 more for the four generations between Inachos and Crotopos, since he allows 100 years for every three generations[b]. Thus, if he regarded the Olympiad of Iphitos as the Olympiad of Corœbos in 776 B.C.[c], he must have placed the Exodus in 1667 B.C., the beginning of this Sothic period in 1322 B.C., and the beginning of the next in 139 A.D.

The earlier date is adopted by Theon of Alexandria in a computation of the risings of the dog-star, where he counts back 1605 years from the Era of Diocletian in 284 A.D., and thus arrives at 1322 B.C.[d]. He calls this date the Era of Menophres: but that does not suffice to place the date in history, for Menophres is unknown.

Clement seems to have assigned the Exodus to the reign of Amosis, as he makes him a contemporary of Inachos of Argos[e]. But in fixing the Exodus at 1667 B.C., he relies on such a series of fabulous events that he cannot be trusted in giving that date to Amasis or Amosis, the first king of Dyn. 18.

The cycle of the dog-star is noted in the Old Chronicle at the end of Dyn. 15[f], and in the Book of the Sothis at the end of Dyn. 16[g]. In this it is assigned to 3475 A.M., and thus stands 1461 years before the accession of the second Amasis in 4936 A.M. The Old Chronicle reckons 1516 years from the end of Dyn. 15 to the end of Dyn. 26; and therefore 1461 years to the accession of Amasis, supposing that it counts his reign as 55 years[h]. And thus these statements

---

[a] Cf. Iliad, xxiv. 765.

[b] Clemens Alexandrinus, stromateis, i. 21. 136, εἰς μέντοι τὰ ἑκατὸν ἔτη τρεῖς ἐγκαταλέγονται γενεαί.

[c] Cf. Pausanias, viii. 26. 4.

[d] A fragment of Theon, printed in Larcher's Histoire d'Hérodote, vol. 2, p. 556, ed. 1802, and also in Biot's Recherches sur plusieurs points de l'astronomie Égyptienne, pp. 303, 304, ἐπὶ τοῦ ρ´ ἔτους Διοκλητιανοῦ περὶ τῆς τοῦ Κυνὸς ἐπιτολῆς ὑποδείγματος ἕνεκεν λαμβάνομεν τὰ ἀπὸ Μενόφρεως ἕως τῆς λήξεως Αὐγούστου. ὁμοῦ τὰ συναγόμενα ἔτη ͵αχε´. οἷς ἐπιπροσθετοῦμεν τὰ ἀπὸ τῆς ἀρχῆς Διοκλητιανοῦ ἔτη ρ´. γίνονται ὁμοῦ ἔτη ͵αψε´.

[e] Clemens Alexandrinus, stromateis, i. 21. 101.

[f] Syncellos, p. 51.　　　　[g] Syncellos, p. 103, cf. pp. 91, 210.

[h] Cf. Diodoros, i. 68. 6.

about the cycle of the dog-star may be connected with the passage in Tacitus about the appearance of a phœnix in the time of Amasis[a]. Indeed the statement in the Sothis may be connected with his notice of the appearance of a phœnix in the time of Sesosis, if this Sesosis is Sesonchis; for the Sothis replaces Sesonchis by Concharis in Dyn. 22, and also introduces Concharis in Dyn. 16 in speaking of this cycle.

These statements would carry Dyns. 15 and 16 back to about 2000 B.C. But they cannot be severed from their context. And the Old Chronicle allows no more than 443 years for the first fifteen Dynasties, while the Sothis puts king Menes, the founder of Dyn. 1, only 700 years before the end of Dyn. 16.

Such statements as these about Dyns. 15 and 16, and also those of Clement and Theon as to 1322 B.C., can only have been based on theories of chronology; for they will not answer to the facts. The dog-star did not really rise at intervals of exactly 365¼ days; and consequently the cycle did not really amount to four times 365¼ years, or 1461. A period that ended at Alexandria in 139 A.D. would really have begun there in 1318, not in 1322 B.C. And further south, at Thebes and Elephantine, the beginning and the ending would both have been considerably later, as the date of rising varies with the latitude.

This all looks as though the cycle was invented by the later Greeks at Alexandria. Nor is there anything to indicate that it was known to the Egyptians in earlier times; no mention of it being found in their inscriptions or papyri, though occasionally these note the risings of the dog-star.

In a calendar, written on the back of a papyrus[b], the rising of the dog-star is placed on day 9 of month 11 in year 9 of king Ser-ka-Ra. This is presumably king Ser-ka-Ra Amen-hetep of Dyn. 18; and he came to the throne in 1249 at latest[c]. Had there been 365 days to the year, day 9 of month 11 would have been 57 days from day 1 of month 1 in

[a] See above, page 53.
[b] University Library, Leipzig. Ebers, Papyros Ebers, plate 1 verso.
[c] See above, page 45.

the year after; and then year 9 of king Ser-ka-Ra would have been assignable to 1550 B.C., that being four times 57 years before 1322 B.C., the supposed date of the rising of the dog-star on day 1 of month 1. But this calendar proceeds from day 9 of month 12 to day 9 of month 1 just as it proceeds from day 9 of any other month to day 9 of the next; so that it clearly is intended for the year of 360 days with twelve months of thirty days apiece and nothing added. And thus it will not serve to fix the date of king Ser-ka-Ra Amen-hetep, as there is nothing to fix the date at which the dog-star rose on day 1 of month 1 in these years of 360 days apiece.

In a fragment of a calendar, inscribed upon a block[a] belonging to a large inscription, the rising of the dog-star is placed on day 28 of month 11. With a year of 365 days, this would put the rising 38 days before day 1 of month 1; and thus it might be taken to refer to 1474, that being four times 38 years before 1322 B.C. But there is nothing in the fragments of this calendar to show whether the year had 365 days, or only 360; and as the fragments came from Elephantine, the calendar was probably intended for a southern latitude in which the time would not be reckoned from 1322. In any case, however, this calendar is useless as a guide to history, since it cannot be assigned with certainty to any king. It doubtless was inscribed upon a building of king Men-cheper-Ra Thothmes: but it may have been inscribed there by one of his successors.

The year of 360 days was still retained for purposes of ritual in the time of Diodoros, certain priesthoods making the 360 libations for the 360 days of the year[b]. According to the Book of the Sothis[c], the five additional days had been inserted by a king named Aseth, who reigned next before Amasis, the founder of Dyn. 18. Plutarch, however, tells another story, saying that the god Hermes won a seventieth part of every day from the goddess Selene, and then joined the bits together into five entire days to make a year of 365.

[a] Louvre. Lepsius, Denkmaeler aus Aegypten, part 3, plate 43. e.
[b] Diodoros, i. 21, 97.   [c] Syncellos, p. 123.

But as Selene was the goddess of the moon, this legend is probably a story of the lunar year of 354 days and its connexion with the year of 360[a].

An elaborate table of the risings of the stars is comprised in the inscriptions in the tombs of kings Neb-mat-Ra Rameses and Nefer-ka-Ra Rameses[b]. This makes the dog-star rise at hour 12 of the night in the middle of month 1, at hour 11 at the beginning of month 2, at hour 10 in the middle of month 2, at hour 9 at the beginning of month 3, and so on. The dog-star would thus have risen at hour 1 of the morning at the beginning of month 1; and as this table makes the year begin with hour 1 of the night at the beginning of month 1, it seems to treat the hour 1 as zero. Had the hours been reckoned from sunset and sunrise, the dog-star would have risen with the sun, when it rose at hour 12 of the night: and would thus have been invisible at rising. Yet it certainly was supposed to be visible then, for the table indicates its place on the horizon; and this hour 12 must therefore have been earlier than sunrise. So the probabilities are that the dog-star rose with the sun, when it rose at hour 1 of the morning; its true rising being thus assigned to the beginning of the year.

In an inscription of the great User-mat-Ra Rameses the rising of the dog-star is associated with the beginning of the year[c]; and so also in an inscription of User-mat-Ra Rameses Heq-Annu[d]. The second of these inscriptions cannot be less than 28 years later than the first, and may be considerably later; seeing that there must have been an interval of 28 years between the reigns of these two kings, and that the first of them reigned for 67 years and the second for 32[e]. Neb-mat-Ra Rameses reigned after User-mat-Ra Rameses Heq-Annu, and Nefer-ka-Ra Rameses reigned after Neb-mat-Ra[f].

---

[a] Plutarch, de Iside et Osiride, 12.

[b] Bab el-Moluk. Lepsius, Denkmaeler aus Aegypten, part 3, plates 227, 228 bis.

[c] Ramesseum. Lepsius, ibid., part 3, plate 170.

[d] Medinet Habu. Champollion, Monuments de l'Égypte, notices, vol. i., p. 370.

[e] See above, pp. 37, 43.   [f] See above, pp. 35, 36.

So this series of inscriptions will cover a space of time in which the date of rising would have changed perceptibly, had the year been limited to 365 days : and yet they seem to keep the date of rising quite unchanged. Possibly, they represent a type of year that was maintained for purposes of ritual, regardless of the actual times of rising. But otherwise they can only mean that the Egyptians had already introduced a year of 365¼ days, or groups of three years of 365 with one of 366.

Thus, there is very little hope of correcting any dates in history by reference to the cycles of the phœnix and the dog-star, or other things pertaining to the calendar. And there is still less hope of learning anything at all from the orientation of the temples.

No building can be planned in such a way as to prevent its axis from pointing to some heavenly body at some date or other; and unless there is some evidence to show that a building was intended to point to some particular body in the sky, nothing can be gained by finding out the date at which it pointed to that body. In the case of the Egyptian temples, the evidence seems to be confined to the buildings of the Ptolemies and Roman Emperors ; and even here it does not really touch the point. These inscriptions[a] state that, when a monarch was laying a foundation stone, he was to face the north, fixing his gaze upon the constellation of the Meschet, or Great Bear. But this only determines the position of the monarch while laying the foundations, and does not show the axis of the building.

---

[a] For example, the inscriptions at Edfu in the Zeitschrift fuer Aegyptische Sprache und Alterthumskunde for 1870, pp. 154, 155.

V.

The Connexion of Egypt with Greece.

Supposing that dates can be determined for the kings of Egypt as far back as the opening of Dyn. 18, there is then a question whether any of these dates can be connected with the early history of Greece. And that depends on evidence of very little weight.

1. The cartouches of king Neb-mat-Ra Amen-hetep and his wife, queen Thii, appear upon a group of things discovered at Mycenæ itself and in a Mycenæan tomb at Ialysos in Rhodes. And this Amen-hetep came to the throne in 1163 at latest[a].

A scarab from Ialysos has a cartouche with *Neb-mat-Ra*[b]; and a scarab from Mycenæ has a cartouche with *Thii*[c]. A fragment of a porcelain vase, also from Mycenæ, has the end of a cartouche with *hetep heq Uast*[c]—apparently the end of the name Amen-hetep with the title 'Lord of Thebes,' which was adopted by Neb-mat-Ra Amen-hetep. And a fragment of a porcelain plaque, also from Mycenæ, has *ta anch* and part of a cartouche with *neb mat;* while another fragment has *se Ra* and part of a cartouche with *Amen*[c]. When put together and completed, these fragments give the

[a] See above, page 44.

[b] British Museum. Furtwaengler and Loeschcke, Mykenische Vasen, plate E, fig. 1.

[c] Polytechnic, Athens. Ἐφημερὶς Ἀρχαιολογική, 1887, plate 13; 1888, page 156; 1891, plate 3.

names and adjuncts *ta-anch Neb-mat-Ra se-Ra Amen-hetep*. But curiously the *ta* and *anch* are upside down; and although the *neb* and *mat* are upright, they come at the wrong end of the cartouche, and the cartouche itself is terminated by a bar at top as well as bottom.

The presence of these cartouches is a proof that the things cannot be earlier than the reign of Neb-mat-Ra Amen-hetep, but not a proof that they are anywhere near so early. Things of this sort could be decorated with a king's cartouche long after his decease. And even supposing that the things in question were made in Egypt in the reign of Neb-mat-Ra Amen-hetep, there is nothing whatever to show that they were brought to Ialysos and Mycenæ at that period. Obviously, they may have been brought over long after they were made. And thus they cannot be taken as an indication of the date of Mycenæan civilization in Greece.

If the Mycenæan antiquities of Ialysos could be attributed to the time of Dyn. 18 on the ground that they include a scarab with the cartouche of Neb-mat-Ra Amen-hetep, the later Greek antiquities of Camiros could be attributed to the time of Dyn. 4 on the ground that they include a scarab with the cartouche of Chufu [a].   And that would be absurd.

Had there been any traffic between Greece and Egypt in the Mycenæan period, this traffic would hardly have begun and ended in a single reign. The probabilities are that, if the Mycenæans had brought things over from Egypt in the reign of Neb-mat-Ra Amen-hetep, they would have brought things over in the reigns of some of his predecessors or successors. Yet his cartouche and his wife's are the only cartouches that have come to light on Mycenæan sites in Greece.

Possibly, the Mycenæans took an interest in this king and queen ; and thus selected things with their cartouches. The king was renowned among the later Greeks as Memnon, their Vocal Memnon being his colossus [b].   And his fame would

---

[a] Louvre.   Revue Archéologique for 1863, vol. 8, p. 2.

[b] Pausanias, i. 42. 3 ; Corpus Inscriptionum Græcarum, vol. 3, nos. 4719—4761 ; C. I. Latinarum, vol. 3, nos. 30–66.

perhaps have reached Mycenæ through his marriage with Thii, who was probably a foreigner[a].

2. Terra-cotta vases of a certain type are discovered in Greece on most of the sites that were inhabited in the Mycenæan age; and occasionally they come to light in Egypt in surroundings that may serve to fix their date. False-necked vases belonging to this class are depicted in fresco in the tomb of king User-mat-Ra Amen-meri Rameses Heq-Annu[b]; and this is a proof that they were known in his time, say 1000 B.C.[c] But obviously they may have come into use long before then, and remained in use long after.

One of them was found at Der el-Bahari with the coffin of a man, who was described in the inscription as a son of the high priest Tchet-Chensu-af-anch, a son of Pinetchem the high priest and king[d]. And as Pinetchem came to the throne in 876 at latest[e], this grandson of his may have died about 850.

On the other hand, five of them were found at Gurob in the same deposit with a broken kohl-tube bearing a cartouche with *neb* and part of *mat*; and several others in the same deposit with some pendants bearing a cartouche with *Neb-cheperu-Ra*[f]. These are presumably the cartouches of kings Neb-mat-Ra Amen-hetep and Neb-cheperu-Ra Tut-anch-Amen. And this Amen-hetep came to the throne in 1163 at latest, and Tut-anch-Amen in 1127 at latest[g].

a See below, pp. 68, 69.

b Bab el-Moluk. Description de l'Égypte, antiquités, vol. 2, plates 87, 92; Champollion, Monuments de l'Égypte, vol. 3, plates 258, 259; Rosellini, Monumenti dell' Egitto, vol. 2, monumenti civili, plate 59; Prisse d'Avennes, Histoire de l'art Égyptien, atlas, vol. 2, plate 84.

c See above, page 37.

d British Museum. No. 22,821. With it were found:—No. 22,822, pilgrim-bottle of white glazed terra-cotta. No. 22,825, wooden box (without lid) in form of a hippopotamus. No. 22,826, four-handled vase (with lid) of blue glazed faience. No. 22,872, large scarab of opaque blue glass, without inscription or device. The coffin itself has disappeared.

e See above, page 31.

f Ashmolean Museum, Oxford, and British Museum. Petrie, Illahun, Kahun and Gurob, pages 16, 17 and plate 17.

g See above, page 44.

These kings' cartouches are not enough to mark the
kohl-tube and the pendants as products of their reigns; for
obviously a king's cartouche could be employed long after his
decease. And in any case the kohl-tube and the pendants
may have been retained in use through many generations
before they finally were buried with these vases. On the
other hand, the coffin of king Pinetchem's grandson must
have been inscribed and buried within a few months of its
owner's death. And thus there are somewhat stronger
grounds for giving the date 850 to the vase discovered with
the coffin than for giving any dates near 1163 and 1127 to
the vases discovered with the kohl-tube and the pendants.

A sample of another class of Mycenæan vases was discovered at Kahun in the same tomb with several scarabs
bearing a cartouche with *Men-cheper-Ra*[a]. That is presumably the cartouche of king Men-cheper-Ra Thothmes of Dyn.
18; and he came to the throne in 1229 at latest[b]. A couple
of these scarabs were in a coffin at the further end of the
tomb, while the vase was in a coffin that blocked the passage
to this end. Hence the coffin with the vase must have been
buried after the coffin with the scarabs, and perhaps a long
while after. These scarabs may have been buried a long
while after they were made. And the cartouches are not
enough to show that they were made so early as the time of
Men-cheper-Ra Thothmes.

A somewhat similar vase[c] was discovered at Saqqarah in
a tomb that dates from the reigns of kings User-en-Ra An
and Tat-ka-Ra Assa of Dyn. 5[d]. But apparently the tomb
had been employed for burials in later ages.

Some hundreds of fragments of Mycenæan vases were
discovered at Tell el-Amarna in company with some dozens
of broken rings, scarabs, etc., bearing the cartouches of various

---

[a] Ashmolean Museum, Oxford. Petrie, Illahun, Kahun and Gurob, pages 22,
23 and plate 26, fgs. 2, 4, 44. Journal of Hellenic Studies, vol. 11, plate 14, fg. 1.
   [b] See above, page 45.
   [c] Berlin Museum. Catalogue, no. 1244. Furtwaengler and Loeschcke,
Mykenische Vasen, plate 22, fg. 159.
   [d] Saqqarah. Lepsius, Denkmaeler aus Aegypten, part 2, plates 60–64 bis.

kings from Men-cheper-Ra Thothmes, who came to the throne
in 1229 at latest[a], to Neb-cheperu-Ra Tut-anch-Amen, who
came to the throne in 1127 at latest[b]: among them, king
Neb-mat-Ra Amen-hetep and his wife, queen Thii, and es-
pecially king Nefer-cheperu-Ra Amen-hetep (or Chu-en-Aten)
and the members of his family[c].

No less than 1329 of these Mycenæan fragments were
found upon a piece of ground outside the limits of the ancient
city, while only 12 were found inside, 9 of them in one place
and 3 in another[d]. And no less than 750 fragments of
Phœnician glass were found upon this piece of ground, while
only 38 were found elsewhere; the whole 38 being in the
neighbourhood of the 9 Mycenæan fragments[d]. On the other
hand, the same excavations brought to light at least 160
fragments of Egyptian terra-cotta vases with inscriptions that
refer to Neb-mat-Ra Amen-hetep, Thii, Chu-en-Aten, and
others of that family[e]: but none of these were found upon
that piece of ground outside the limits of the ancient city.

Thus, in order to maintain the notion that these Mycenæan fragments are contemporary with those kings of Dyn. 18,
one must suppose that when the people broke a vase of coarse
Egyptian ware, they left the fragments lying about promis-
cuously; but when they broke a vase of delicate Mycenæan
ware or even of Phœnician glass, they carried the fragments
out of the city and threw them away upon this piece of
ground outside. And that does not seem likely.

In digging up this piece of ground the soil was found to
be quite shallow, the depth being about a foot upon the
average and nowhere more than four feet; and there was
nothing whatever to indicate that the Mycenæan and Phœnician fragments were thrown away there at the same date
with the broken rings and scarabs. The city was the favourite
residence of Chu-en-Aten; and for many years past its site
has been treated as a mine for relics of this king and his
associates in Dyn. 18.

[a] See above, page 45.   [b] See above, page 44.
[c] Petrie, Tell el Amarna, pages 15, 16 and plates 14, 15, 26–30.
[d] Ibid., page 16.   [e] Ibid., plates 21–25.

T.   5

In the same way a quantity of foreign pottery was found at Kahun upon a piece of ground outside the limits of the ancient city; and this pottery was intermixed with Egyptian remains of the time of king Cha-cheper-Ra Usertesen of Dyn. 12[a]. He came to the throne in 1346 at latest[b]. The pottery, however, is mainly of the types that come to light at Naucratis and other places occupied by Greeks between 700 and 500. And this shows the futility of arguing that things must date from the same period, if they happen to be discovered in the same deposit.

3. The inlaid daggers from Mycenæ[c] are somewhat in the style of a dagger that was found near Der el-Bahari with the coffin of queen Ah-hetep. This dagger[d] has the cartouches of queen Ah-hetep's son, king Neb-pehtet-Ra Ahmes of Dyn. 18; and he came to the throne in 1271 at latest[e]. But, assuming that this dagger is really of his time, its resemblance to the Mycenæan daggers is scarcely close enough to mark them as contemporary.

Another of these daggers has come to light at Thera, an island that is celebrated for its vases of the Mycenæan age[g]. But this dagger bears no greater likeness to the dagger of king Ahmes.

4. In the frescos in the tomb of Rech-ma-Ra[h] four groups of foreigners are depicted with offerings in their hands for

[a] British Museum. Petrie, Illahun, Kahun and Gurob, page 9 and plate 1. Journal of Hellenic Studies, vol. 11, plate 14, figs. 5-10.

[b] See above, page 51.

[c] Polytechnic, Athens. Bulletin de correspondance Hellénique, vol. 10, plates 1-3. Perrot and Chipiez, Histoire de l'art dans l'Antiquité, vol. 6, plates 17-19.

[d] Gizeh Museum. Catalogue, no. 951. Revue générale de l'architecture for 1860, vol. 18, plate 4-6, figs. 18, 19. Birch, Fac-similes of the Egyptian relics discovered at Thebes in the tomb of queen Aah-hotep, plate 1.

[e] See above, page 45.

[f] Copenhagen Museum. Mémoires des Antiquaires du Nord for 1880, plate 8.

[g] See below, appendix, pp. 70 ff.

[h] Abd el-Qurnah. Wilkinson, Manners and customs of the ancient Egyptians, vol. 1, plate 2, ed. 1878. Prisse d'Avennes, Histoire de l'art Égyptien, atlas, vol. 2, plates 75, 76. Mémoires de la Mission Archéologique Française, vol. 5, pages 33, 36 and plates 5, 7—cf. page 202 and plate 1 for similar subjects in the tomb of Men-cheper-Ra-seneb.

presentation to king Men-cheper-Ra Thothmes; and in two of these groups the presents include a number of metal vases of Mycenæan shapes and also several daggers. This king came to the throne in 1229 at latest[a]. But the manufacture of such articles may have flourished for centuries in the districts whence these came, beginning long before his time and continuing long after. And neither the Mycenæan vases found in Greece, nor yet the Mycenæan daggers, need therefore be contemporary with those depicted in these frescos.

The people who are bringing the vases and the daggers, are described in the inscriptions as the princes of the land of Keftu and the islands in the great sea, and the princes of the land of Retennu and all the lands beyond. In the Greek version of the hieroglyphs in the Canopic decree of 238 B.C.[b] the names Keftu and Retennu are translated as Phœnicia and Syria; and they seem also to bear this meaning in inscriptions of earlier date. The islands that are grouped here with Keftu or Phœnicia, were presumably the string of islands along the Phœnician coast, which were occupied by the Phœnician cities, Tyre, Sidon, Arvad and the rest. And the places grouped with Retennu or Syria, were presumably at no great distance from that country.

This perhaps may indicate that the Mycenæan antiquities in Egypt were brought there from the parts about Phœnicia; and that, although the Egyptians and the Mycenæans may both have trafficked with that country, they need never have come in contact with each other.

In the Canopic decree[c], the Rosetta stone[d], etc., the name Hellenes is translated as Haui-nebu; and that name is found in inscriptions as far back as the time of kings Teta and Pepi of Dyn. 6[e]. But this is not a proof that the Egyptians were acquainted with the Hellenes at any remote date. The name Haui-nebu means 'Lords of the North'; and although this

[a] See above, page 45.
[b] Gizeh Museum. Lepsius, Das bilingue Dekret von Kanopus, plate 2, line 9 and plate 5, line 17.
[c] Gizeh Museum. Lepsius, ibid., plate 4, line 37 and plate 8, line 74.
[d] British Museum. Lepsius, Auswahl, plate 18, line 14 and plate 19, line 54.
[e] Saqqarah. Recueil de travaux for 1884, vol. 5, pp. 37, 161, 177.

suited the Hellenes in the time of the Ptolemies, in earlier
times it would have suited other races.

There are really no grounds at all for identifying the
Achæans with the Aqaiuasha. That tribe is mentioned in
inscriptions of king Ba-en-Ra Mer-en-Ptah[a], but not in those
of any earlier or later kings. He came to the throne in 1028
at latest[b]. According to his inscriptions, the Aqaiuasha and
other tribes had made their way into the Delta, and they
were defeated there by the royal troops in the fifth year of
his reign. They are described in these inscriptions as people
of the land of the sea; but this can only mean that their
home was on the sea-coast in the neighbourhood of Egypt,
for the narrative shows that the invaders came by land.
And thus there is nothing, beyond an accidental likeness in
the names, to justify the notion that the Aqaiuasha were
Achæans. Nor is there anything in other records to connect
the Egyptians with the inhabitants of Greece in the Mycenæan
age.

The only cartouches that have come to light on Mycenæan
sites in Greece, are those of king Neb-mat-Ra Amen-hetep
and his wife, queen Thii[c]. And on one of the large scarabs of
this king and queen, with a date in year 10 of his reign, the
statement is that Thii was a daughter of Iuaa and Thuaa;
and that Kirgipa, a daughter of prince Satharna of Naharna,
had then arrived in Egypt[d]. In the cuneiform despatches of
king Tushratta of Mitani to king Nibmuariya, or Neb-mat-Ra,
greetings are sent to Tii, or Thii, and also to Gilukhipa, or
Kirgipa, whom Tushratta calls his sister[e]. Mitani, or Mathen,
is mentioned between Naharna and Retennu in a list of the
conquests of king User-mat-Ra Rameses Heq-Annu[f]; and

---

[a] Karnak.   Mariette, Karnak, plate 52, lines 1, 14, plate 54, lines 52, 54.
Gizeh Museum.   Zeitschrift fuer Aegyptische Sprache und Alterthumskunde for
1883, page 67, line 13.

[b] See above, page 43.   [c] See above, pp. 61, 62.

[d] Zeitschrift fuer Aegyptische Sprache und Alterthumskunde for 1880, p. 82.

[e] British Museum.   Bezold and Budge, The Tell el-Amarna Tablets, no. 9.
Berlin Museum.   Winckler and Abel, Der Thontafelfund von El-Amarna, nos.
23, 24.

[f] Medinet Habu.   Duemichen, Historische Inschriften, vol. 1, plate 17.

between Keftu and the islands in a list of those of king Men-cheper-Ra Thothmes[a]. And thus, supposing that the names of Thii's parents mark her as a foreigner, the probabilities are that she came from the same region with those foreigners who brought the daggers and vases of Mycenæan types as offerings to this Thothmes. In that case the things with Thii's cartouches and her husband's may have reached the Mycenæan sites in Greece by transit through this region : the inference being that they did not find their way there because they named the reigning king and queen, but because they named a king and queen in whom the people of that region took a patriotic interest.

Upon the whole, the evidence that points to intercourse, direct or indirect, between Greece and Egypt in the Mycenæan age, points to a period that began in 1271 at latest[b] and ended in 850 or thereabouts[c]. This evidence, however, is all of very little weight; and there is evidence that tends to contradict it. For example, the Greek coins and gems of about 700 to 600 resemble the Mycenæan gems so closely, that any judge of art would be prepared to place the Mycenæan age immediately before 700. But whatever weight be given to such evidence as this, there certainly is nothing to justify the confident assertion that the Mycenæan age in Greece was concurrent with Dyn. 18 in Egypt, and that this Dynasty began in 1700.

---

[a] Gizeh Museum. Mariette, Karnak, plate 11, lines 16—18.
[b] See above, page 66.   [c] See above, page 63.

APPENDIX.

The Vases from Thera.

Some vases of Mycenæan type have been discovered on the island of Thera in the Ægean Sea ; and their date is said to be fixed at about 2000 B.C. by geological evidence. This geological evidence is given in *Santorin, et ses éruptions*, by M. F. Fouqué, who took a leading part in the discovery of the vases.

These vases were all found underneath the pumiceous tufa —not underneath the lava, as has sometimes been asserted. M. Fouqué thought at first that some of them had been found above this tufa, and said so in the *Archives des missions scientifiques*[a]: but he discovered afterwards that this was a mistake, and put it right in his book[b].

In M. Fouqué's opinion, the whole of this pumiceous tufa is composed of the pumice that was ejected in prehistoric times from a gigantic cone, which formerly covered the bay between the twin islands of Thera and Therasia. Therefore, he argues, the vases were in existence before the collapse of the cone. And thus, to determine the date of the vases, we must ascertain when the cone collapsed. To this problem he addresses himself, but *avec de grandes réserves*. His views are expressed in almost the same words on pp. 249-251 of the *Archives* and on pp. 129-131 of his book. His principal argument runs thus :—

" Le premier fait sur lequel je m'appuierai est emprunté à l'observation des îlots du centre de la baie. Après l'effondrement et les terribles phénomènes qui

---

[a] Series 2, vol. 4, pp. 243, 249, 250, &c.   [b] Page 108.

l'avaient précédé, il y a eu certainement une longue période d'assoupissement : c'est seulement 196 ans avant J. C. qu'une éruption nouvelle a produit l'îlot nommé Palæa-Kaméni. A partir de cette date, des éruptions successives ont eu lieu pendant les premiers siècles de l'ère chrétienne et ont agrandi l'îlot nouvellement formé. Une seconde période de calme relatif a rempli tout le moyen âge, et ce n'est qu'à partir du quinzième siècle que les éruptions ont repris leur fréquence et leur énergie, et engendré de nouveaux îlots. La seconde période de calme ayant eu une durée de dix siècles environ, on peut, sans témérité, attribuer à la première une durée minima double de celle-ci, surtout quand on compare l'intensité si différente des phénomènes volcaniques auxquels ils ont succédé. D'après cette considération, la formation de la baie remonterait à environ deux mille ans avant J. C."

Now, that is not geology, but a mixture of geology and history : and the history is wrong.

An island was upheaved in the bay between Thera and Therasia in 196 B.C. This upheaval is described by Strabo[a] and by Seneca[b]; both authors getting their materials from the lost work of Poseidonios. The exact date is fixed by Justin[c] and Plutarch[d], as they associate the event with the overthrow of Macedon by Rome in 196 B.C.

Another island was upheaved there in 46 A.D. This upheaval and its date are mentioned by Seneca[e], by Dion Cassius[f], and by Aurelius Victor[g].

Possibly, there had been another upheaval between 196 B.C. and 46 A.D. According to the present reading[h], Pliny says that an island was upheaved there in the fourth year of Olympiad CXXXV. This should certainly be CXXXXV, for the fourth year of that Olympiad was concurrent with 196 B.C. He says that another island was upheaved there in the consulship of M. Junius Silanus and L. Balbus. They were consuls in 19 A.D.; but M. Junius Silanus was one of the consuls in 46 A.D. Pliny cannot have omitted the upheaval in 46 A.D. from his notice of these islands : so he must be referring here to 46 A.D., but inadvertently assigning the wrong colleague to Silanus. He says also that another island was upheaved 130 years after the former and 110 years before

[a] Strabo, i. 3. 16.   [b] Seneca, quæstiones naturales, ii. 26.
[c] Justin, xxx. 4.   [d] Plutarch, de Pythiæ oraculis, 11.
[e] Seneca, quæstiones naturales, ii. 26, vi. 21.   [f] Dion Cassius, lx. 29.
[g] Aurelius Victor, de Cæsaribus, 4.   [h] Pliny, ii. 89.

the latter; and thus in 66 or 65 B.C. But his statement is not corroborated; and Seneca says explicitly that the island of 46 A.D. was the second.

There was a terrific eruption with another upheaval in 726 A.D. or thereabouts. This is described by Nicephoros Patriarches[a] and Theophanes Confessor[b], and also by Cedren[c].

Thus there were upheavals in the bay in 196 B.C. and 46 A.D. and 726 A.D., and perhaps about 65 B.C. also; but in the intervals the volcano was quiescent. Consequently, there is no foundation for M. Fouqué's opinion that there was a period of activity beginning in 196 B.C. and lasting through the early centuries of the Christian era, and then a period of quiescence for about a thousand years, ending in the fifteenth century. After the eruption of 196 B.C. come two periods of quiescence, of 241 and 680 years respectively; or if the time from 196 B.C. to 46 A.D. be reckoned as a period of activity, the following period of quiescence amounts to only 680 years, and this is followed by another period of quiescence of about the same length. Now, even supposing that the period of quiescence before 196 B.C. was twice as long as the period of quiescence after 46 A.D., the cone did not collapse until about 1556 B.C.; or if this period before 196 B.C. was twice as long as the period next after that date, the cone did not collapse until about 678 B.C. But there does not appear to be any valid reason for supposing that the first of these periods was twice as long as the second, as M. Fouqué suggests. He is of opinion that the volcano was far more violent before the first period than before the second, and therefore required this longer time to rest. But that can only be a matter for speculation.

A second argument is adduced by M. Fouqué, and this is strictly geological. At the northern point of Therasia the pumiceous tufa was covered with a thick bed of stones intermixed with sea-shells. A period of fully 1000 or 1200 years would have been required for the formation and elevation of

---

[a] Nicephoros Patriarches, p. 37.   [b] Theophanes Confessor, pp. 338, 339.
[c] Cedren, p. 454.

this bed. And this process must have been complete before the eighth century B.C., for there were ancient buildings upon this bed with inscriptions which probably date from that century. Consequently, the pumiceous tufa must have been formed here about 2000 B.C. at latest.

This argument rests on the opinion that 1000 or 1200 years were needed for this purpose. And that, again, can only be a matter for speculation.

M. Fouqué holds that the pumiceous tufa below these buildings must be contemporary with the pumiceous tufa above the vases, since the whole of the pumiceous tufa on Thera and Therasia is composed of pumice that was ejected from the former cone above the bay during one vast eruption. That opinion he supports in this way :—

" D'abord nous pouvons démontrer que la grande éruption ponceuse a précédé l'effondrement du centre de l'île, car le tuf qui couvre les falaises actuelles de Théra et de Thérasia est coupé à pic comme les laves sous-jacentes, ce qui ne peut s'expliquer qu'en supposant qu'il a été entaillé par l'effondrement tout comme le reste."

It is true that the cliffs of Thera and Therasia, which face the bay, exhibit a vertical section of the strata composing them, and that at the top there is a stratum of pumiceous tufa which is cut off abruptly like the others. But this will not suffice to prove that this stratum was there before the cone collapsed and left the present face of the cliff exposed to view.

Pumice was ejected from the new cone in the bay during the eruption of 196 B.C. The fact is mentioned by Seneca[a]. And during the eruption of 726 A.D. pumice was ejected in enormous quantities. According to Theophanes[b] it covered the Ægean Sea and extended to Asia Minor, the Dardanelles, and the south of Macedonia.

But if pumice was ejected then in such abundance as to cover the Ægean and reach places more than 200 miles from

[a] Seneca, quæstiones naturales, ii. 26.
[b] Theophanes Confessor, pp. 338, 339, πετροκισήρους μεγάλους ὡς λίθους τινὰς ἀναπέμψαι καθ' ὅλης τῆς Μικρᾶς Ἀσίας καὶ Λέσβου καὶ Ἀβύδου καὶ τῆς πρὸς θάλασσαν Μακεδονίας, ὡς ἅπαν τὸ πρόσωπον τῆς θαλάσσης ταύτης κισήρων ἐπιπολαζόντων γέμειν.

Thera and Therasia, vast masses must have fallen on the islands themselves: and these masses of pumice must be represented by some portion of the stratum of pumiceous tufa which now covers the upper surface of the islands.

In attributing the whole of the pumice to one vast eruption in prehistoric times, M. Fouqué has taken no account of the eruptions in historic times. Yet these eruptions must be responsible for part of the pumiceous tufa at the top of the cliffs; and if a part of that stratum was formed after the collapse of the cone, the whole of that stratum may have been formed after the collapse, though it certainly is cut off very abruptly towards the bay. Apart from the fact that the stratum is cut off abruptly, no facts are adduced by M. Fouqué in support of his opinion that all the pumiceous tufa on the islands is composed of pumice ejected from the cone that afterwards collapsed.

In short, M. Fouqué's theory is that the vases must date from about 2000 B.C. at latest, since they were found underneath pumiceous tufa formed from the pumice ejected from a cone which collapsed about 2000 B.C. But, in the first place, he does not give very satisfactory reasons for fixing the date of the collapse anywhere near 2000 B.C. And then, in the second place, he altogether fails to show that the pumiceous tufa which covered the vases, need have been formed from the pumice ejected from this cone.

CAMBRIDGE: PRINTED BY J. AND C. F. CLAY, AT THE UNIVERSITY PRESS.

By the same Author.

Ancient Ships. *Illustrated.* Demy 8vo. 1894. 10s. 6d.

Independent research, erudition without pedantry, and a respectable knowledge of modern seamanship and nautical terminology are conspicuous merits of this treatise.—*Times.*

Parla egli delle navi a remi ed a vela, delle loro dimensioni, dei materiali impiegati, degli alberi, delle vele, della pittura, del timone, dei dipinti di prora e di poppa, delle ancore, gomene, bandiere, fanali, scandagli, battelli, ecc., ecc., in una parola, di tutti gli attrezzi e le particolarità inerenti alla forma ed armamento marinaresco d' una nave a remi ed a vela, corroborando le sue speditive affermazioni con un ricco e sovratutto ben scelto e corretto materiale di citazioni originali, desunte dagli storici e poeti greci e latini.—*Rivista Marittima.*

Das Verdienst des Verfassers liegt in der selbständigen und umfassenden Sammlung und Verzeichnung der auf seinen Gegenstand bezüglichen literarischen Überlieferung aus dem Alterthum. Sie reicht von Homer bis auf die Byzantiner und Kirchenväter und bietet beträchtlich mehr auch als die ausführlichsten älteren Werke.—*Literarisches Centralblatt.*

On y trouvera un exposé un peu sec et dogmatique, mais précis et appuyé sur un solide échafaudage de textes et de monuments, de tout ce qui touche à la structure proprement dite et à l'équipement des navires antiques : rames, dimensions et tonnage, matériaux, coque, ancres, câbles, gouvernail, mâture, signaux, tous ces sujets sont traités successivement avec une singulière maîtrise des documents et un esprit critique fort aiguisé.—*Revue des Études Grecques.*

His book contains the results of long, laborious, and careful research. It is a scholarly work, and brings to the surface a vast amount of useful information hitherto scattered on the bottom of the ocean of ancient history.—*New York Times.*

Rhodes in Ancient Times. Demy 8vo. 1885. 10s. 6d.

Eine recht fleissige Monographie über die Insel Rhodos, bei der die in den Ausgrabungen zu Tage gekommenen kunstarchäologischen Fundstücke sowohl wie die massenhaften Inschriften verarbeitet worden sind.—*Berliner Philologische Wochenschrift.*

Rhodes in Modern Times. Demy 8vo. 1887. 8s.

Le sujet était intéressant et nouveau ; il a été traité avec soin et une connaissance peu commune des historiens de Byzance.—*Revue Critique.*

London: C. J. CLAY AND SONS,
CAMBRIDGE UNIVERSITY PRESS WAREHOUSE,
AVE MARIA LANE.
Glasgow: 263, ARGYLE STREET.

The Cambridge University Press.

—

Illuminated Manuscripts in Classical and Mediæval Times, their Art and their Technique, by J. H. MIDDLETON, Litt.D., Director of the Art Museum at South Kensington. With Illustrations. Royal 8vo. Buckram, 21s.

A Descriptive Catalogue of the Manuscripts in the Fitzwilliam Museum. Illustrated with Twenty Pages of Photographic Reproductions. By MONTAGUE RHODES JAMES, Litt.D., Director of the Fitzwilliam Museum and Fellow of King's College. Royal 8vo. Buckram, 25s. *Net.*

Greek Coins, Types of, by PERCY GARDNER, Litt.D., F.S.A., late Disney Professor of Archæology. With 16 Autotype Plates, containing photographs of Coins of all parts of the Greek World. Impl. 4to. Cloth extra, £1. 11s. 6d.; Roxburgh (Morocco back), £2. 2s.

Pheidias, Essays on the Art of, by C. WALDSTEIN, Litt.D., Phil.D., Slade Professor of Fine Art in the University of Cambridge. Royal 8vo. With numerous Illustrations. 16 Plates. Buckram, 30s.

The Origin of Metallic Currency and Weight Standards. By W. RIDGEWAY, M.A., Disney Professor of Archæology in the University of Cambridge, and late Fellow of Gonville and Caius College. With Illustrations. Demy 8vo. 15s. *Net.*

The Mummy: Chapters on Egyptian Funereal Archæ- ology. By E. A. WALLIS BUDGE, Litt.D., F.S.A., Keeper of the Department of Egyptian and Assyrian Antiquities, British Museum. With numerous Illustrations. Demy 8vo. 12s. 6d.

A Catalogue of the Egyptian Antiquities in the Fitz- william Museum. By E. A. WALLIS BUDGE, Litt. D., F.S.A. 10s. 6d.

Sophocles. The Plays and Fragments with Critical Notes, Commentary, and Translation in English Prose, by R. C. JEBB, Litt. D., LL.D., Regius Professor of Greek in the University of Cambridge. Demy 8vo.

Part I. **Oedipus Tyrannus.** *Third Edition.* 12s. 6d.

Part II. **Oedipus Coloneus.** *Second Edition.* 12s. 6d.

Part III. **Antigone.** *Second Edition.* 12s. 6d.

Part IV. **Philoctetes.** 12s. 6d.

Part V. **Trachiniae.** 12s. 6d.

Part VI. **Electra.** 12s. 6d.

Part VII. **Ajax.** [*In the Press.*

———

London: C. J. CLAY AND SONS,
CAMBRIDGE UNIVERSITY PRESS WAREHOUSE,
AVE MARIA LANE.
Glasgow: 263, ARGYLE STREET.

www.ingramcontent.com/pod-product-compliance
Lightning Source LLC
Chambersburg PA
CBHW022012050726
47499CB00007BA/2548